PEACE IN THE WORKPLACE

PEACE IN THE WORKPLACE

Transforming Conflict Into Collaboration

Robyn Short

GoodMedia Press, Dallas, TX

GoodMedia Press

An imprint of goodmedia communications, llc

25 Highland Park Village, 100-810

Dallas, Texas 75205

www.GoodMediaPress.com

Cover design by Lindsey Bailey

Book design by GoodMedia Press

The text in this book is set in Cambria and Futura

Manufactured in the United States of America

Names: Short, Robyn, author.

Title: Peace in the workplace : transforming conflict Into collaboration / Robyn Short.

Description: Includes bibliographical references. | Dallas, TX: GoodMedia Press, 2016.

Identifiers: ISBN 978-0- 9911148-2- 5 | LCCN 2013954424

Subjects: LCSH Conflict management. | Personnel management. | Organizational change. | Organizational effectiveness.| Leadership. | BISAC BUSINESS & ECONOMICS / Strategic Planning | BUSINESS & ECONOMICS / Workplace Culture | BUSINESS & ECONOMICS / Conflict Resolution & Mediation | BUSINESS & ECONOMICS / Leadership

Classification: LCC HM1126 .S76 2016 | DDC 303.6/9--dc23

For Scott

CONTENTS

PREFACE

Peace is not the absence of conflict, but rather a state of navigating conflict nonviolently while respecting the human dignity of all people.

PEACE. IT IS NOT RAINBOWS and unicorns — something reserved exclusively for hippies and lovers of the liberal arts. Peacemakers are brave; they are tough and uncompromising when it comes to doing what is right.

Peace in the workplace is not a lofty goal; it is a human right. On Dec. 10, 1948, the United Nations adopted the Universal Declarations of Human Rights, which was drafted by representatives with different legal and cultural backgrounds from all regions of the world, to recognize the inherent dignity of the "equal and inalienable rights of all members of the human family" and to make known that these rights are "the foundation of freedom, justice and peace in the world." Article 23 of the Universal Declaration of Human Rights asserts the following:[1]

1. Everyone has the right to work, to free choice of employment, to just and favorable conditions of work and to protection against unemployment.
2. Everyone, without any discrimination, has the right to equal pay for equal work.
3. Everyone who works has the right to just and favorable remuneration ensuring for himself and his family an

existence worthy of human dignity, and supplemented, if necessary, by other means of social protection.

4. Everyone has the right to form and to join trade unions for the protection of his interests.

These rights do not come easily to most Americans and certainly not to most individuals around the world. To create peace and be a protector of peace takes courage and resolve. But first and foremost, it requires the knowledge of these rights and the understanding of how to achieve and protect them.

So, if "peace" is not rainbows and unicorns, then what is it? Peace is human security — justice, equality and the ability to live a life of dignity that is free of fear. If peace does not seem to have a role in the workplace, then consider what it may be like to be:

- Bullied in the workplace
- Sexually harassed in the workplace
- Paid unequally by market standards and/or as compared to peers
- Discriminated against due to sexual orientation, ethnicity or religion
- Forced to comply with unethical or illegal requests by a superior for fear of retaliation
- Compelled to hide a pregnancy for fear of losing a job or not being able to secure one
- Exposed to near constant, unmanaged and unresolved workplace conflict

PREFACE

Anyone who has experienced one or more of the above conflicts understands that these experiences prevent a person from achieving safety and freedom from fear. They are also barriers to justice — defined as access to opportunities that allow a person to achieve his or fullest potential — and equality.

Conflict is extraordinarily prevalent in the workplace. According to one study that analyzed workplace conflict in nine countries, 85 percent of the 5,000 survey respondents indicated they deal with conflict to some degree. In the United States, 36 percent of employees claim to spend a significant amount of time managing disputes — 2.8 hours a week to be exact, which results in more than one full day per month.[2] Conflict, in and of itself, does not equate to a lack of peace, but it can lead to a lack of peace when it is poorly managed. Research shows that 27 percent of employees have seen conflict erupt into personal attacks, and 25 percent of employees report that avoidance of conflict resulted in illness or a decision to stay home from work.[3]

Poorly managed conflict, or conflict that is not managed at all, can wreak havoc on productivity, employee engagement and an organization's ability to get work done. But most importantly, it can be a significant catalyst for the violation of human rights. And that is the purpose of this book: to provide organizational leaders, board members, shareholders, employees and volunteers with an understanding of the concept of peace and how to achieve it in the workplace.

CHAPTER ONE

THE NEUROSCIENCE OF PEACE BUILDING

CREATING NEURAL PATHWAYS FOR COLLABORATION

For the first time in human history, people have access to the knowledge, skills and intellectual capability to choose their destiny by intentionally shaping their own individual development rather than reactively evolving to changes in their environment.

DESTRUCTIVE CONFLICT IN THE WORKPLACE is most likely not a result of people choosing to cause harm, but rather individuals causing harm because they have not developed the tools to behave differently. The brain is a powerful tool, yet individuals who do not have a basic understanding of the brain become victims of their own lack of understanding. For the uninformed, evolutionary coping mechanisms for survival are the autopilot responses to conflict. Whether conflict is being experienced at home or in the workplace, creating peace requires a basic understanding of the brain so as to respond to conflict intentionally rather than instinctively.

Humans have existed on Earth and have been in a process of continuous change for more than 200,000 years, and the modern form of humans has been evolving for more than 50,000.[4]

This process of evolution and continuous change has largely been a result of humans adapting to changes in the environment. In other words, external forces served as the catalyst for human evolution. Historically, humans have been reactive rather than proactive in their development, changing because the environment around them changed. Continuous change served as a mechanism for survival — adapt to the evolving environment or risk extinction. However, for the first time in human history, humans now have the knowledge, skills and intellectual capability to choose their destiny by intentionally shaping their own individual development rather than reactively evolving to changes in their environment. Internal forces, rather than external forces exclusively, can now serve as the catalyst of human development.

The 20th and 21st centuries ushered in an unprecedented understanding of the human brain, and with this understanding of the brain came a deeper understanding of human behavior: what shapes how an individual thinks and, therefore, behaves; what shapes "group think" and, therefore, how the individuals that make up a group behave. Advances in neuroscience demonstrate that humans are not puppets living under the mysterious control of some unknown force but rather *are* that force and have great power in shaping the future of it. To understand how humans can intentionally shape their own development and assert greater control over their behavior requires an understanding of the brain — the anatomy of it and how it works — so as to become more cognitively deliberate and intentional in their actions.

THE ANATOMY OF THE BRAIN

The brain is an exceptionally sophisticated organ responsible for regulating thoughts, memory — and the interconnected relationship between the two — judgment, personal identity and other aspects collectively referred to as "the mind." However, the brain's responsibilities do not stop there. It also regulates all aspects of the body — voluntary and involuntary. It is both the birthplace of hopes and dreams and the engine that allows for the creation and realization of them. The brain and spinal cord comprise the nervous system — the hub for processing and communicating the information that controls all aspects of the human body.[5]

The forebrain, midbrain and hindbrain are the three main parts that comprise the brain. The cerebrum, which comprises the left and right hemispheres of the brain, the brain stem, which is attached to the spinal cord, and the cerebellum, which is located below and behind the cerebral hemispheres are important structures within the forebrain, midbrain and hindbrain.[6]

The Cerebrum

The cerebrum is the largest section of the brain. This portion of the brain plays a critical role in decision-making. Understanding the cerebrum and how it works is paramount to the intentional shaping of human development. From an evolutionary perspective, this is a highly developed area of the brain and can be thought of as the brain's CEO. The cerebrum is where complex functions such as action and thought occur. Housed within the cerebrum are the following:[7]

- The **frontal lobe** is often referred to as the "executive center" of the brain because it controls cognition, including speech, planning and problem-solving. It contains an important area of the brain called the prefrontal cortex, which is responsible for foreseeing consequences of actions, exercising self-restraint and developing moral and ethical standards.

- The **parietal lobe** controls sensation (i.e., touch, pressure and ascertaining size and shape).
- The temporal lobe mediates visual and verbal memory as well as smell.
- The **occipital lobe** controls visual reception and the recognition of both shapes and colors.

Each of these lobes is divided by sulci — fissures that form boundaries between each. The cerebrum is symmetrical in structure and is divided into left and right hemispheres. Generally, the left hemisphere is responsible for functions such as creativity, and the right hemisphere is responsible for functions such as logic and spatial perception. Though each side has distinct areas of control, they are interdependent of one another. Every human has a dominant hemisphere that controls language, mathematical and analytical functions, as well as whether that person is left-handed or right-handed. The non-dominant hemisphere controls simple spatial concepts, facial recognition, some auditory functions and some emotional functions. Nerve fibers send messages to the body, crossing over the medulla; therefore, the left hemisphere controls the right side of the body and the right hemisphere controls the left side of the body.[8]

The limbic lobe is comprised of adjacent portions of the frontal, parietal and temporal lobes that surround the corpus collosum and is involved in both involuntary and voluntary behavioral activities, receiving input from the thalamic nuclei that are connected with parts of the hypothalamus and with the hippocampal formation.[9]

The basal ganglia — large gray masses of nerve cells called nuclei — exists within the cerebral hemispheres. There are four basal ganglia:

1. The caudate
2. The putamen
3. The global pallidus
4. The amygdala

From an evolutionary perspective, the amygdala is the oldest of the basal ganglia and is almost exclusively concerned with survival. The amygdala controls the "fight, flight and freeze" response designed to ensure the body has the hormonal support necessary to respond when the brain perceives a life-threatening stimulus. The amygdala is an almond-shaped nucleus located under the corpus striatum in medial parts of the temporal lobe. While the amygdala does receive olfactory input as a function of its survival responsibilities, it plays no role in olfactory perception.[10]

Beneath the cerebrum and above the brainstem is the diencephalon. This portion of the brain is comprised of the epithalamus, thalamus, hypothalamus (responsible for controlling the sex drive, pleasure, pain, hunger, thirst, blood pressure, body temperature and other body functions such as the emission of oxytocin) and the subthalamus. The diencephalon functions as a relay system between incoming sensory input and other areas of the brain and is also a location for interaction between the central nervous system and endocrine system. The diencephalon has a role in the limbic system — the area of the brain located below the cerebrum and in front of the cerebellum — which is responsible for hereditary traits, emotions and memories. The limbic system also has a role in regulating basic body functions.[11]

The thalamus plays an important role in the relay and distribution of most sensory and motor signals to specific regions of the cerebral cortex. The thalamus segregates and organizes the sensory signals, which are generated in numerous receptors and projected via intricate pathways to specific relay nuclei. Just below the thalamus lies the hypothalamus, which controls the endocrine functions such as the secretion of oxytocin — an important hormone associated with bonding, developing trust and forming human attachments — and vasopressin, a hormone that allows for the muscle contractions of the reproductive and digestive systems.[12]

The Brain Stem

While the cerebrum is the engine of thinking and emotions, the brain stem is the engine for basic body functions. It is the area of the brain that works "behind the scenes" and on autopilot, keeping the body breathing, pumping blood and managing critical functions that keep the body alive. The brain stem includes:[13]

- The **midbrain** — controls visual and auditory systems
- The **pons** — controls arousal and respiration and serves as a relay system for the cerebrum and cerebellum

- The **reticular activating system** — a group of nerves concerned with consciousness and alertness

The Cerebellum

The cerebellum, sometimes referred to as the "little brain," regulates and coordinates nerve impulses between the brain and the body's muscles. Playing no role in sensory perception, the cerebellum is concerned with influencing the body's ability to maintain equilibrium, muscle tone and the coordination of voluntary motor control.[14]

HOW THE BRAIN WORKS

Communication within the nervous system largely occurs between independent cells — one cell transferring information to another. There are two types of cells: neurons and neuroglia (also referred to as glial) cells. The neurons are the "task masters" of the brain while the glial cells work as the "body guards" for the neurons. The brain consists of more than 10 billion neurons, all of which have their own identities expressed in complex networks of unique relationships with other neurons.[15]

Neurons are the brain's carriers of information. Much like a cargo ship transports goods from one port to another, neurons carry data from one area of the brain to another. All actions — voluntary and involuntary, conscious and unconscious — derive from the transmission of information from one neuron to another, a process called neurotransmission.

A neuron consists of a cell body that has branching structures called dendrites. These branching structures reach out of the cell body in the same way that tree branches reach out from the trunk. The dendrites receive information from nearby neurons in the form of impulses and push that information through the cell body in which they are associated. The neuron also has an axon — a tube-like fiber with its own branching system — that carries nerve impulses away from the cell body to the dendrites of nearby neurons. The axon of one neuron reaches out to the dendrite of another neuron, but they do not actually transport information by touching. Rather, there is a space between the two called a synapse. Neurons translate their messages into presynaptic and postsynaptic chemical messages. The chemical floats out of the presynaptic neuron and is caught by the postsynaptic. The chemical message fits into the receptor like a key in a lock, and that is where the message is translated. These chemical messengers are called neurotransmitters. The neurotransmitters float across the synapse to communicate with the second neuron. The neurotransmitter is then either recycled back into the presynaptic neuron, or it can be dumped into the synapse and flushed out into the cerebral spinal fluid.[16]

Neurotransmitters Involved in Human Connectivity

Extraordinarily complex and highly intricate, the brain has developed numerous chemicals, including hormones and neurotransmitters, to strengthen or weaken responses and to influence how information is organized. The following chemicals are particularly relevant to human connectivity:[17]

- Adrenalin — triggers the fight/flight/freeze response
- Testosterone — stimulates aggression

- Oxytocin — instills trust, increases loyalty and promotes attachment and bonding
- Estrogen — triggers the release of oxytocin
- Endorphins — reinforces collaborative experiences with pleasure
- Dopamine — generates a reward response and fortifies addiction
- Serotonin — regulates moods
- Phenylethylamine — induces excitement
- Vasopressin — encourages bonding in males

Each of the above mentioned chemicals influences how the brain responds to conflict and attachment, yet humans are not enslaved to these chemicals. There is choice involved. How a person chooses to respond to a conflict situation or an opportunity for human connection will inform the brain on the appropriate chemical response and how much of that chemical is necessary to achieve the desired response.

Neural Pathways

Because all actions and functions of the human mind and body are the result of neurotransmissions, the brain has developed efficiencies in the form of neural pathways. Much like a well-worn path is created by constant travel, neural pathways develop within brain structures that allow certain actions to go on autopilot. For example, simple activities such as tying one's shoe, brushing one's teeth, making coffee and even more complex tasks that are done routinely such as operating complicated machinery or driving a car are all actions the brain has developed sophisticated and "well-worn" pathways for, allowing a person to complete these tasks without giving any conscious thought to them. These neural pathways free the brain to give more energy and focus to other neural networks that are not as well formed. For example, while making coffee, one may be thinking about a complicated task that needs to be completed later in the day that requires solutions that have yet to be determined. The solutions-focused thinking involves the connecting (wiring and firing) of numerous neurons as information is delivered to various areas of the brain that are necessary to accomplish the task. One neural network is working on autopilot while another is actively forming.

Understanding this in relation to mundane tasks such as tying one's shoes or making coffee is easy, but the same "autopilot" concept holds true to belief systems about one's self, one's family of origin, one's community, one's coworkers and the belief systems associated with politics, religion, the environment, work and how work should be conducted, etc. The brain does not discriminate against right and wrong, moral and immoral, healthy and unhealthy, productive and unproductive, collaborative and competitive. The brain is a brilliant order-taking machine that simply creates what it is asked to create, and it is very efficient about creating what it is asked most frequently to create. This is great news when a person's neural pathways are life sustaining, promote positive human connection, develop and perpetuate trust, bonding and attachment. But when the neural pathways are founded in self-interest at the expense of others, zero-sum expectations regarding resources, or fear-based responses to differing ideologies and belief systems, then these efficiencies the brain so brilliantly developed can become destructive to self, the community, coworkers and, ultimately, humanity.

CREATING NEURAL PATHWAYS FOR PEACE AND COLLABORATION

In order to consciously create neural pathways designed for peace, collaboration and a mindset of sustainability of all life, one must have an understanding of the anatomy of the brain, how the brain functions and the key areas of the brain that help to form specific emotions, feelings and behaviors. In order to change something, one must understand what is being tasked to change.

The human brain is wired for survival. To that point, it is designed for two main functions: 1) keep the individual alive; and 2) keep the species alive. All areas of the brain support one another to create opportunities for the human and the human species to remain in existence.

Emotions serve as an important evolutionary tool to ensure survival, which is why the brain experiences two primary emotions: fear and love. All feelings, at their core, are founded in one of these two emotions. When one of these two emotions is triggered, the nervous system responds with chemicals that create numerous feelings that inform human behavior.

From a neuroscience perspective, there is a distinct difference between emotions and feelings. Emotions are physiological and can be objectively measured by blood flow, brain activity, facial microexpressions and body language. Feelings are how the individual expresses emotions.

Feelings are based off memory associations and reactions the individual has with that emotion. Feelings are subjective and are influenced by personal experiences, beliefs, personal temperament and memories. The emotion of fear may be expressed in the following feelings:

- Anger
- Hatred
- Disgust
- Anxiety
- Panic

While the emotion of love may be expressed by these feelings:

- Calm
- Happy
- Comfort
- Connected
- Safety

Mirror neurons play an important role in the expression of emotions. Mirror neurons are a class of brain cells that fire when an individual performs an action and also when the individual observes someone else performing the same action.[18] Because connectivity is paramount to human survival, humans are intensely social beings. Mirror neurons send messages to our limbic system allowing us to experience what others feel. They allow for the deepening of prosocial behavior because they give individuals the ability to have intensely shared emotional experiences. For example, watching someone perform deeply emotional music inspires a shared emotional experience. Observing an individual crying often brings tears to the eyes of the observer. Watching someone experiencing a panic attack causes panic in the observer. Mirror neurons are the birthplace of empathy and suggest that deep within the human architecture is the framework for connectivity or "togetherness." There would be no point of a mirror neuron system if humans were designed to live in isolation from one another.[19]

The Amygdala

As mentioned previously, the amygdala is, from an evolutionary perspective, the oldest of the basal ganglia and is almost exclusively concerned with survival. Located deep within the anterior inferior temporal lobe, it receives information from the sensory regions of the thalamus and the cortex as well as from the hippocampus and prefrontal cortex.[20] The amygdala plays a critical role in the survival of the human species because it is the guardian of the fear emotion and provides the body with the chemicals — most notably adrenaline — to respond to life-threatening stimuli.[21] The connections from the amygdala to the cortex can influence the attention the brain gives to a perceived threat, which is influenced by both the perception of the current stimuli as well as memories of previous perceptions of danger. The amygdala also has indirect influence over the cortex through its connections to the attention system in the brainstem, which has other parts that trigger the cascade of physiological reactions associated with fear that send feedback to the brain. The "in the moment" feedback merges with the feedback associated with working memory to produce the unique feelings associated with an emotion.

When the brain receives a sensory stimulus that informs it that danger is present or pending, that information is routed to the thalamus. The thalamus routes it over two parallel pathways: the thalamo-amygdala pathway (the "short route") and the thalamo-cortico-amygdala pathway (the "long route"). The thalamo-amygdala pathway conveys a quick, high-level impression of the situation that does not involve cognition. This pathway activates the amygdala and generates an emotional response before any perceptual integration has had time to occur. However, the information that travels through the thalamo-cortico-amygdala pathway is processed in the cortex and informs the amygdala on the validity of the threat. The assessment requires various levels of critical processing, including a comparison of explicit memory by means of the hippocampus, which communicates closely with the amygdala. The hippocampus supports explicit memory and holds information about the dangerousness of a situation or object. The hippocampus is especially sensitive to context associated with behaviors that have been negatively perceived. The hippocampus is responsible for a stimulus (and the objects and conditions surrounding the stimulus) becoming a long-term source of conditioned fear. This perception of imminent danger activates the amygdala. The parallel operation of the explicit (hippocampal) and implicit (amygdalic) memory systems explains why traumas experienced very early in childhood are often not remembered. The hippocampus is not yet fully developed during childhood, but the amygdala is well formed and ready to record unconscious memories. Early childhood traumas can disturb the mental and behavioral functions of adults by providing inaccurate data upon which to act.[22] This data, whether accurate or not, plays a critical role in the development of neural pathways — pathways that shape behavior.

In a truly life-threatening situation, the amygdala can be a real lifesaver. However, as noted previously, memory can provide false data. Without intervention from the prefrontal cortex — the executive center of the brain tasked with logic and analytical thinking — the amygdala can cause the individual to behave in self-destructive behaviors. For example, if a child is lost at the park and cannot find his parent, he may experience an intense feeling of panic that causes him to freeze in one place. The chemicals flooding his body may literally have rendered him frozen in fear. This can be a very pro-survival response to danger because it might give the parent an enhanced opportunity to find the child. Fast-forward 20 years, and that fear may have become so profound that it was imprinted in the brain as: "being alone is dangerous." However, the person is incapable of remembering the source of the fear because of his underdeveloped hippocampus at the time of the event. The memory can persist for decades, or perhaps throughout his life. He may feel a great sense of discomfort, or even full-blown panic attacks, when he is alone — at home or in the workplace. This fear may cause great disruption in his day-to-day life as he seeks out every opportunity to avoid what might, as an adult, be understood as "co-dependent." This is an oversimplified example of how the amygdala can provide a false sense of danger to the brain that, without intervention, can cause self-destructive behavior. Apply this same thinking to false data about individuals of other cultures, ethnicities, belief systems, work ethics, etc., and it quickly becomes apparent how self-destructive neural pathways can develop and perpetuate behavior that is self-destructive to both individuals — personally and professionally.

This process of feeling overtaken by fear is referred to as an "amygdala hijack" — when the amygdala is engaged, and the fight/flight/freeze coping mechanism is activated. In a truly life-threatening situation, the amygdala hijack may save a person's life. But when a person is hijacked inappropriately, such as when experiencing conflict that violates any one of the inherent human rights or when conflict such as workplace bullying persists for long periods of time, the mental, emotional and physical stress can create a ripple effect of conflict that spreads far and wide throughout an organization, creating secondary and tertiary conflict. Chapter 3 will present techniques to prevent and/or intervene an amygdala hijack.

Repeated traffic through a select trail of grass eventually creates a clearly defined pathway. Neural pathways are the same. The more an individual perpetuates a thought or belief system, the more developed the neural pathway becomes. In other words, the more "true" it becomes to the individual. And, just like the well-worn path, a lack of use results in new growth covering the previous pathway, which means the path through the grass is not destined to always be a path. A lack of wear allows it to take on a new shape. The same holds true about belief systems. Intervention allows a new pathway to take shape. New information changes previously held belief systems and forges new pathways that inform different behaviors. Neuroscience has brought to the forefront of human possibility the awareness that the past does not have to shape the future. New neural networks can be developed at any time by seeking out and consuming new information, then acting upon that new information in order to allow pathways for different behavior to emerge.

In his book, *The Dance of Conflict: Explorations in Mediation, Dialogue and Conflict Resolution Systems Design*, author Kenneth Cloke surfaces the poignant reality that, "While people in conflict commonly make reference to the facts, behaviors, feelings, personalities or events surrounding their conflicts, for the most part they ignore the deeper reality that these experiences are all processed and regulated by their nervous systems, and are therefore initiated, resolved, transformed and transcended by their brains."[23] In other words, individuals create, process and experience conflict and are, therefore, solely responsible and completely capable of processing information differently. The brain can remain mired in conflict or it can transcend it.

The Hypothalamus

Just as the amygdala is the guardian of the emotion of fear and activates the "fight, flight or freeze" response to perceived threats, the hypothalamus is associated with oxytocin — the prosocial, "tend and befriend" hormone that encourages trust, increases loyalty and promotes attachment and bonding. Oxytocin is primarily in the hypothalamus. From there, it is either released into the blood stream via the pituitary gland or to other parts of the brain and spinal cord where it attaches to oxytocin receptors thereby influencing behavior and physiology.[24] While the fundamental features of living are contingent upon the activities of the entire brain, the hypothalamus plays an important role in maintaining the body's comfort by maintaining homeostasis — the maintenance of hormone emission, body temperature, blood pressure, heart rate, water and electrolyte levels.[25]

Research shows that oxytocin may have a dual purpose and dual pathways. When an individual is experiencing periods of low stress, oxytocin physiologically reinforces good social bonds with feelings of well-being. However, when a person is experiencing periods of high stress and high levels of the stress hormone cortisol are present, oxytocin can encourage prosocial behavior such as seeking out the positive attention and affection of others.[26]

The hormone oxytocin — and the catalysts for its emission in the body — supports the notion that the human brain is wired for connectivity. Actual or anticipated social contact can cause bursts of oxytocin emission. However, the brain may also respond to the stress associated with periods of social deficits with bursts of oxytocin emissions in order to produce physiological changes that then encourage the individual to behave in more prosocial ways — i.e., a physiological nudge to make positive contact with other people. In this manner, oxytocin actually affords the potentially stressful experiences to become an opportunity for expressing kindness and joy.[27]

Research has found oxytocin to be an incredible resource for powerfully increasing trust. Numerous studies have found that participants who are given pretend money and then encouraged to invest that money with a stranger will, on average, invest only one-fourth to one-third of their money. However, after a few sniffs of oxytocin, their trust levels increase significantly and their investment amount jumps to 80 percent or more.[28] There is a reciprocal relationship between oxytocin and empathy: Oxytocin increases an individual's capacity for empathy, and empathy increases the emission of oxytocin in the body. Therefore, from an evolutionary perspective, it is beneficial to exercise empathy in relationship to others because both the act and the hormone serve to strengthen social bonds.

According to Daniel Goleman, author of *Emotional Intelligence: Why It Can Make You Smarter Than IQ*, explains the three types of empathy in an article posted to his website:[29]

1. **Cognitive empathy**: Cognitive empathy is knowing how another person feels, or "perspective-taking." This form of empathy is highly effective at motivating people to apply their best efforts. While at first blush all forms of empathy may appear to be prosocial, cognitive empathy does have a dark side. Individuals who are purely self-motivated (such as interrogators, narcissists and sociopaths) can be masters at this form of empathy and utilize it for purely selfish reasons.

2. **Emotional empathy**: Emotional empathy is truly feeling the emotion along with another individual. Emotional empathy is due to the activation of mirror neurons, which help individuals to be attuned to another person's inner emotional world. While emotional empathy does promote bonding and attachment and can positively affect trust and loyalty, one downside is that it can become overwhelming to the person extending empathy, causing burnout and

then ultimately detachment as a coping mechanism. Emotional empathy must be paired with a healthy ability to self-regulate one's own emotions and high attention to self-care.

3. **Empathetic empathy**: Empathetic empathy, also referred to as empathic or compassionate empathy, involves the capability of understanding a person's predicament and feeling with them along with the willingness to help if necessary. This form of empathy is what the emotion love looks like in action.

NEUROSCIENCE AND HUMAN DEVELOPMENT

An intentional and widespread focus on increasing empathy and collaboration is paramount in order to achieve peace, justice and equality in the workplace. For the first time in human history, individuals are able to lay claim to a peaceful existence through collaborative means rather than reacting to changes aggressively and competitively. Neuroscience presents the knowledge necessary to master the human mind and, therefore, human behavior.

Knowledge is the key to change. In order to change the human brain, the human brain must be understood by the masses, and the power each individual person has to affect great change within his or her own mind must be understood by all — or at least by enough individuals to create the tipping point effect. Strategies for creating neural pathways for peace and collaboration include:

- Creating change within one's self
- Learning to cultivate empathy
- Learning and implementing conflict resolution techniques

All of the above stimulate and perpetuate new neural pathways in the brain.

Create Change Within Oneself

To transcend adversaries in the external world, one must first transcend the adversaries within one's internal world. To do this requires implementing practices and tactics designed to develop new, prosocial neural networks that support peaceful resolution for conflict and enhance the release of oxytocin.

In his book, *Conflict Revolution: Designing Preventative Solutions for Chronic Social, Economic and Political Conflicts,* mediator and peace builder Kenneth Cloke advises on many small, practical and deeply personal ways every person can participate in systemic change, by being the very change they wish to see in the world and certainly the workplace:[30]

- Be open, honest and willing to communicate fearlessly so as to surface rules coworkers operate under but have not declared, unspoken or secret expectations, and covert behaviors
- Listen closely and empathetically, especially to individuals who hold differing opinions

- Act with unconditional integrity and respect, giving generously of one's self without expecting anything in return
- Increase sensitivity toward the emotional, cultural systems and processes of coworkers and the work environment
- Be inclusive with people and groups who have not previously been included
- Rethink the definitions and parameters of success and failure
- Invite open, honest and empathetic feedback while giving more generously of one's self
- Offer feedback, evaluation and assessment using collaborative and democratic methods
- Be willing and open to apologizing, forgiving and surrendering in order to build trust and create a team that is stronger, better, smarter and more productive than the sum of its individual members

In addition to the tactics listed above, meditation is also a powerful form of reducing stress, the second most prevalent source of conflict in the workplace, and achieving inner peace so that one may be an agent of peace outwardly. Many companies are embracing meditation and mindfulness practices in order to bring about more positive work environments. Companies such as Google, Aetna, General Mills, Intel, Target and Green Mountain Coffee Roasters all offer mindfulness programs to employees. Participants of these programs report feeling less stressed, have increased focus and clarity, increased thinking and decision-making skills, as well as an improved sense of overall well-being.[31] Research also shows that mindfulness-based practices help to improve social relationships, increase the body's immune system, allow for more positive and effective responses to stress and optimize emotional regulation.[32]

Mindfulness training is a particularly effective method for achieving inner peace because it involves the practice of "re-perceiving." Mindfulness practices train the individual to become an observer to his or her life story by developing awareness of personal narratives, much like a mirror reflects an image without being immersed in it. The ability to observe one's narratives brings about a profound shift in the relationship one has with his or her thoughts, emotions and feelings, resulting in greater clarity, perspective and objectivity. The profound shift that is experienced is, in part, due to the fact that the brain structure in individuals who meditate quite literally changes. The area of the insula — which involves interoceptive and visceral awareness and may also play a role in the process of awareness — shows marked difference in individuals who meditate as compared to those who do not.[33]

Another important reason mindfulness practices enhance feelings of inner peace is because they involve the teaching of acceptance. An important component of meditation and other mindfulness practices is the acceptance of physical sensations, emotions and feelings, and thoughts and judgments, as they are experienced. No meaning is placed on them; they move through the meditator without consideration. Studies show that acceptance is an important element to experiencing inner peace.[34]

There are numerous forms of mindfulness practices, including numerous varieties of sitting and walking meditations, yoga, journaling and prayer, all of which serve as powerful tools for creating and sustaining neural pathways for peace and collaboration.

Cultivate Empathy

While empathy is something some people experience and express in higher degrees than others, it is something all people can cultivate and practice in daily life. The following are just a few techniques to help cultivate empathy in the workplace. Chapter 2 provides an in-depth exploration of communicating with honesty and empathy.

- **Active listening**: Active listening is a technique in which the listener relays back to the speaker what he or she heard the speaker say by way of restating or paraphrasing what was heard in his or her own words. This serves a dual purpose of confirming the listener correctly heard and understood what the speaker said and also provides the opportunity to verify that it was interpreted accurately. This practice allows the speaker to feel heard and understood and the listener the ability to gain important insight into the emotions and feelings of the speaker, humanizing both parties in the process.

- **Being fully present**: To be fully present means that all focus is on what is happening in the here and now. The individual's intention is focused on noticing what is happening and not trying to control what it is happening. It is being present to the words being spoken, the emotions being experienced and the feelings being expressed without analyzing, judging or placing attachment to them.

- **Taking personal interest**: To take personal interest in another person or in a situation is the epitome of empathetic empathy. Taking a personal interest involves the willingness to be personally invested in the solution and assuming responsibility or joint responsibility in doing so.

Embrace Conflict Resolution Techniques

Workplace conflict provides rich and potentially rewarding opportunities to gain a deeper understanding of one's self and one's coworkers. Understanding how to navigate conflict in such a way that is nonviolent and productive is critical to creating sustainable peace in the workplace. The following are just a few conflict resolution techniques that hold great promise in creating more peaceful work environments as it relates to the nonviolent, interest-based resolution of workplace conflict. Each of these will be explored in greater detail in Chapter 6.

- **Mediation**: Mediation is a form of conflict resolution that invites an impartial third party into a conflict to facilitate a mutual agreement between or amongst all parties. Mediation is designed to empower the parties who participated in the creation of a conflict to also be the authors of it resolution. Interest-based mediation is designed to address the foundational causes of conflict, optimizing collaboration and agreement amongst all involved.

- **Restorative justice**: Restorative justice models seek to repair the harm that has been done to an individual or individuals as a result of another person or persons' behavior(s). Restorative justice models bring those who have been harmed by another's actions into a restorative process designed to reclaim as much normalcy as possible for the person who has been harmed, and allows the person who created the harm to take ownership and responsibility in the repair.

- **Dialogue circles**: Dialogue circles are a safe space created for participants to talk about what is important to them via a facilitated dialogue by a professionally trained facilitator. Dialogue circles are an opportunity to develop respect and trust while sharing in a journey that affects all team members within an organization or perhaps all employees of the organization.

Understanding the basics of neuroscience and having at least a rudimentary understanding of the brain is critical to creating lasting peace in the workplace. In order to bring about lasting and positive change, one must understand the tools with which that change will be created. Neuroscience provides insight into why people behave the way they do in calm and in conflict and, therefore, insight into how one might behave differently. Understanding that humans have the ability to master their thoughts, and therefore their actions, and to shape their human development intentionally and through peaceful and collaborative means gives great promise to the possibilities of creating lasting peace in the workplace.

CHAPTER TWO

COMPASSIONATE COMMUNICATION
CREATING UNDERSTANDING THROUGH
HONESTY AND EMPATHY

Compassionate communication fosters collaboration by establishing relationships
rooted in honesty and empathy.

COMMUNICATION IS THE FOUNDATION FOR how humans relate. Communication is a process of giving and receiving words, sounds, body language, facial expressions, eye movement, tone of voice, etc. A shift in any one of these communication elements can create a shift in how messages are received and experienced, and these shifts inform how those for whom the messages are intended may respond as well as assumptions about their intent.

The previous chapter demonstrates the numerous areas of the brain involved in consuming, processing and responding to the messages received by individuals and the external environment. This chapter provides the information and skills necessary for implementing peaceful communication — communication that engages the frontal lobe (executive center of the brain wired for human connectivity) rather than the amygdala (fight, flight or freeze center of the brain wired for survival). To communicate peacefully requires that a person become conscious to the often habitual and automatic responses of aggression and competition, and consciously and deliberately choose forms of communication that demonstrate respect and empathy toward others and that honor the dignity that is inherent to their humanity.

COMMON RESPONSES TO CONFLICT

To create peace in the workplace — a place where all people can experience justice, equality and a culture free of fear — an understanding of how people respond to conflict and the pitfalls and benefits of each type of response is helpful. In the book *Resolving Conflicts at Work: Ten Strategies for Everyone on the Job*, authors Kenneth Cloke and Joan Goldsmith note, "To shift large-scale personal and organizational attitudes toward conflict, it is necessary that the responses, behaviors, and actions of large numbers of individuals become more conscious, responsible and oriented to learning, resolution and collaboration."[35] The following overview of the most common responses to conflict demonstrates how conflict can be a barrier to peace in the workplace as well as an opportunity for fostering it. Each of the five responses — competing, accommodating, avoiding, collaborating and compromising — demonstrate the different attitudes one holds toward one's self and his or her perceived opponent and the conflict itself.

Kenneth W. Thomas and Ralph H. Kilmann, authors and creators of the Conflict Mode Instrument (TKI) assert that in conflict situations — situations in which the concerns of two people appear to be incompatible — an individual's behavior can be described along two dimensions: (1) assertiveness, the extent to which the person attempts to satisfy his own concerns, and (2) cooperativeness, the extent to which the person attempts to satisfy the other person's concerns.[36] From these two basic dimensions of behavior emerge five different modes for responding to conflict situations:[37]

- **Competing.** Assertive and uncooperative, competing is when an individual pursues his or her own concerns at the expense of others. This is a power-oriented mode in which a person defends his or her position with winning as the ultimate end game.
- **Accommodating.** Unassertive and cooperative, accommodating is the opposite of competing. When an individual accommodates, he or she neglects his own concerns in order to satisfy the concerns of others.
- **Avoiding.** Unassertive and uncooperative, avoiding is when a person neither pursues his or her own concerns nor those of the others so as to not deal with the conflict.
- **Compromising**. Moderately assertive and cooperative, compromising seeks to find a quick or efficient, yet mutually acceptable, solution that partially satisfies all parties. Compromising addresses an issue more directly than avoiding, but fails to explore it as thoroughly as collaborating.
- **Collaborating.** Assertive and cooperative, collaborating is the opposite of avoiding. Collaborating is attempting to work with others in order to find a solution that fully satisfies the concerns of all.

All people are capable of implementing any of the five conflict responses, though it is not unusual for people to utilize one response more frequently than others. The following chart, drawn from Thomas and Kilman's research, reveals how each response relates to concern for people and concern for results.

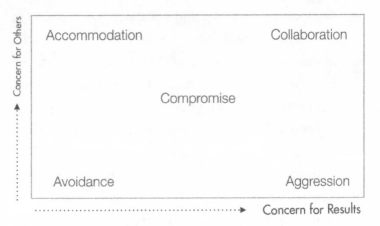

Responding to conflict effectively requires employing each type of conflict response at the right moment, with the right person, to solve the right problem in the right way. Responding to conflict with compassion requires understanding why others may choose a particular response to conflict. In their book, *Resolving Conflicts at Work*, Cloke and Goldsmith offer examples of when one might choose one response over another in any given conflict.[38]

Reasons for Avoiding in Conflict
- The person perceives the issue to be trivial
- The person has no power over the issue or cannot change the results
- The person believes the damage due to conflict outweighs its benefits

- The person needs to cool down, reduce tensions or regain composure
- The person needs time to gather information and cannot make an immediate decision
- The person can leave it to others who are in a position to resolve the conflict more effectively
- The person regards the issue as tangential or symptomatic and prefers to wait to address the real problem

Reasons for Accommodating in Conflict

- The person realizes he or she was wrong or wants to demonstrate the ability to be reasonable
- The person recognizes that the issue is more important to others and want to establish goodwill
- The person realizes he or she is outmatched or losing, and giving in will prevent additional damage
- The person wants harmony to be preserved or disruption avoided
- Reasons for being aggressive in conflict
- The person wants to engage in quick, decisive action
- The person has to deal with an emergency
- The person is responsible for enforcing unpopular rules or discipline
- The person sees the issues as vital and knows that he is right
- The person needs to protect himself against people who take advantage of collaborative behavior

Reasons for Compromising in Conflict

- The person's goals are moderately important but can be satisfied by less than total agreement
- The person's opponents have equal power, and the individual is strongly committed to mutually exclusive goals
- The person needs to achieve a temporary settlement of complex issues
- The person needs a quick solution, and the exact content does not matter as much as the speed with which it is reached
- The person's efforts at either competition or collaboration have failed, and a backup is needed
- Reasons for collaborating in conflict
- The person believes it is possible to reach an integrative solution even though both sides find it hard to compromise
- The person's objective is to learn
- The person believes it is preferable to merge insights that come from different perspectives
- A long-range solution is needed
- Gaining a commitment and increasing motivation and productivity by using consensus decision making is important
- Empowering one or all parties is important
- Working through hard feelings and improving morale is needed
- Modeling cooperative solutions for others is important
- Helping people learn to work closely together is valued

- Resolving the conflict rather than masking the problems is desired
- Involving all parties is an important goal
- Creative solutions are needed
- Nothing else has worked

Collaboration produces the best and most satisfying results, especially when there is an ongoing relationship to consider among all parties such as coworkers, clients and customers. Collaboration does require the highest level of skill and the greatest investment of both time and energy. Collaboration is also paramount to peace in the workplace and is an end result of compassionate communication in the workplace.

COMPASSIONATE COMMUNICATION

Compassionate communication involves expressing what one sees, feels and needs and making requests that enrich one's life based off those three elements with honesty while extending these very same elements of communication to others with empathy. In his book, *Nonviolent Communication: A Language of Life*, author Marshall B. Rosenberg explains, "When we focus on clarifying what is being observed, felt, and needed rather than on diagnosing and judging, we discover the depth or our compassion."[39] Compassionate communication, also referred to as "nonviolent communication," is a specific framework for the expressing of one's self with honesty and receiving the self-expression of others with empathy. This four-part framework is as follows:[40]

1. **Observations:** The concrete actions we observe that affect our well-being
2. **Feelings**: How we feel in relation to what we observe
3. **Needs:** The needs, values, desires, etc. that create our feelings
4. **Requests:** The concrete actions we request in order to enrich our lives

The process of nonviolent communication is not a set formula, but rather a framework that can be adapted to situations as well as personal and cultural styles. The framework is an internal process that may or may not be spoken out loud, but involves giving of one's self in the form of honest self-expression as well as in the form of empathetic receiving. Communication is giving and receiving in a manner that supports human security.

A Framework for Self-Expression

Workplace conflict is caused by numerous sources, but the most common cause of conflict in the workplace — almost 50 percent — is due to warring egos and clashes in personalities.[41] Research commissioned by CPP, Inc., and reported in "CPP Global Human Capital Report: Workplace Conflict and How Businesses Can Harness It to Thrive" found that the following are additional causes of workplace conflict (listed in the order of prevalence):[42]

- Stress
- Heavy workloads
- Poor leadership from the top of the organization

- Lack of honesty and openness
- Poor line management
- Lack of role clarity
- Lack of clarity about accountability
- Clash of values
- Poor selection/pairing of teams
- Taboo topics (e.g., office affairs)
- Poor performance management
- Bullying/harassment
- Perceived discrimination

Each of the above causes of workplace conflict can be transformed by utilizing a framework for communication designed to get at the root causes of the conflict with compassion and an authentic intent for fostering collaboration as the objective rather than alienating, blaming and shaming.

Honest self-expression begins with observation. To observe is to simply identify what is being seen, heard and/or experienced. Observation is not synonymous with evaluation, which is to apply judgment to what is being observed. In his book, *Nonviolent Communication*, Rosenberg identifies three types of evaluations that are particularly alienating and that foster aggression and competition rather than collaboration:

1. Moralistic judgments
2. Comparison judgments
3. Denial of responsibility judgments

Moralistic judgments imply that another person is bad because that person's value system differs from those of the observer. Moralistic judgments are often framed as insults, blames, put-downs, criticisms or labels. Examples of moralistic judgments include: "He is just lazy;" "She thinks she is too good to do real work;" "He's arrogant or stuck-up;" "She's a racist;" etc. This type of language is aimed at finding fault rather than gaining understanding. By judging the person, the underlying reasons for the behavior remain undiscovered, and therefore, the need that is not being met remains undiscovered and misunderstood. Rosenberg explains that, "analyses of others are actually expressions of our own needs and values."[43] In other words, by claiming another person is lazy, the unmet need of the observer might be the need for assistance; by claiming another person is arrogant, the unmet need of the observer might be to experience acknowledgment for a contribution; by claiming another person is racist, the unmet need of the observer might be to have the dignity and respect of all people acknowledged and valued; etc. Expressing values and needs in the form of moralistic judgments increase defensiveness, resistance and, ultimately violence, while decreasing compassion, collaboration and peace.

Comparison judgments block compassion because they create a belief of inferiority about one person and superiority about another rather than a sense of celebration in the unique achievements and contributions of each person. Comparison judgments are put-downs that create feelings of shame, sadness, depression and an overall sense of not being "good enough." Comparison judgments are equally damaging when they are self-imposed as when they are imposed by others. An example of a comparison judgment imposed by others is, "This concept lacks vision and inspiration. You clearly do not have the creative chops Lindsey has." A self-imposed comparison judgment might look something like this, "I feel like such an idiot every time I present in front of the client. My presentation style is not as dynamic or interesting as Lucy's."

Denial of responsibility judgments such as, "You make me feel guilty," "You make me so mad," "I'm just doing my job" or "It's the company policy" incorrectly place the responsibility of one's own feelings and/or actions onto another person or entity. No one has the power or ability to control another person's feelings or emotions. Denying responsibility for one's own feelings or actions implies lack of choice and therefore lack of accountability for one's own thoughts, behaviors and feelings. This type of judgment is dishonest, void of empathy and compassion and is disrespectful and dishonoring to individuals or groups who may have been harmed by the person's actions.

In the book *Sway: The Irresistible Pull of Irrational Behaviors* authors Ori Brahman and Rom Brafman present ideas for what causes people to make irrational decisions which by their very nature can lead to conflict. One such obstacle is the concept of "diagnosis bias." The authors write, "the moment we label a person or a situation, we put on blinders to all evidence that contradicts our diagnosis."[44] Diagnosis bias is the human propensity for labeling people, ideas or things based off an initial evaluative judgment and the challenge to reconsider the judgment once it has been made. One reason diagnosis bias can be so challenging to overcome is because of confirmation bias — another human tendency to seek out information that confirms one's initial judgment or preconceived idea. Humans are quite prone to attributing certain qualities to a person based on their evaluative judgments rather than objective data — this is called value attribution. Once a person perceives another as labeled in a particular way (i.e., lazy, arrogant, smart, ambitious, etc.), the tendency is to take that label at face value. Diagnosis bias, confirmation bias and value attribution are obstacles to overcome in order to observe objectively.

Observation with evaluation is often experienced as criticism, which fosters defensiveness, resentment, anger, sadness, aggression and a host of other feelings, all of which alienate people from one another and fail to create collaborative work environments.

- **Evaluation**: It's really rude that you never arrive to work on time.
- **Observation**: You were late to work 16 times this month.

- **Evaluation**: You think you are too good to actually do the hard work.
- **Observation**: You delegated to other team members three times on this project.

- **Evaluation**: You think I can just read your mind when it comes to your expectations of my role on the team.
- **Observation**: I have not yet received a job description outlining your expectations of me.

- **Evaluation**: You are a bully, and everyone knows it.
- **Observation**: You interrupted me and raised your

voice above the others in the meeting this morning. Several people commented that yours actions caused them discomfort.

- **Evaluation**: You just think your time is so much more important than anyone else's.
- **Observation**: You failed to show up to three meetings last week and did not call or email to let anyone know you would not be attending.

Rather than using observations as opportunities to evaluate and judge behavior, compassionate communication uses observations as opportunities to gather information about concrete actions in order to understand how those actions affect one's own well-being.

The second step to honest self-expression is identifying and expressing one's feelings. Too often in the workplace the idea that "it's not personal; it's just business" is deemed an acceptable approach to workplace communication. All business is conducted by people, which means all business is, in fact, personal. Rather than being perceived as a sign that a person cares deeply about his or her work, a person may be ridiculed or even punished for revealing emotions about his or work. Emotions guide thoughts and actions; therefore, seeking to understand the emotions of others and the feelings they choose to express them should be considered a good leadership skill and a smart business practice. Yet, many cultures, including the American culture, subscribe to the belief that the corporate environment is no place to express feelings; however, the long list of common workplace conflicts demonstrates that feelings matter. They matter greatly. And when feelings are hurt, not honored or left unacknowledged, conflict ensues and collaboration is rendered challenging if not impossible.

Because American culture does not value the expression of emotions, most people have an underdeveloped "feelings vocabulary," meaning most people literally do not have the language to describe their feelings. And the language that does exist is often "feelings prohibitive." Expressing feelings in the workplace is often perceived as weak and unprofessional. Yet, Rosenberg explains, "Expressing vulnerability can help resolve conflicts."[45] And Dr. Brené Brown, University of Houston researcher and professor and author of numerous books including *Daring Greatly* asserts, "Vulnerability is the birthplace of innovation, creativity and change."[46] Vulnerability and attention to feelings is core to connecting with others, and therefore, it is a critical aspect of compassionate communication and workplace collaboration.

Because most people do not have a strong "feelings vocabulary," an explanation of what is a feeling and what is not a feeling is warranted. Chapter 1 provides an overview of the important distinction between emotions and feelings. In his book, *Nonviolent Communication*, Rosenberg makes an important point: "A common confusion, generated by the English language, is our use of the word *feel* without actually expressing a feeling." Very often the word "feel" could, and perhaps should, be replaced with the word "think." For example: "I *feel* I deserved the promotion" is more accurately stated as, "I *think* I deserve the promotion" as it is an opinion that is being expressed rather than a feeling.

Rosenberg offers categories to help differentiate feelings from thoughts. The following are indications of thoughts rather than feelings — although the word "feeling" is used to describe the "thought":[47]

Words such as *that*, *like*, as *if* ...

> I feel *that* you should know better.
>
> I feel *like* a failure.
>
> I feel as *if* I'm living with a wall.

The pronouns *I*, *you*, *he*, *she*, *they*, *it*:

> I feel *I* am constantly on call.
>
> I feel *it* is useless.

Names or nouns referring to people:

> I feel *Amy* has been pretty responsible.
>
> I feel *my boss* is being manipulative.

One must also pay careful attention to distinguish between what one *feels* and what one *thinks* of him or herself. Rosenberg offers the following examples:[48]

Description of what we *think* we are ...

I feel *inadequate* as a guitar player. (This statement is an assessment of ability rather than a description of a feeling.)

Expressions of actual feelings:

> I feel *disappointed* in myself as a guitar player.
>
> I feel *impatient* with myself as a guitar player.
>
> I feel *frustrated* with myself as a guitar player.

Another common mistake people may make when trying to understand their feelings is to confuse the words one may use to describe actual feelings with the words one may use to describe what he or she thinks others are doing. Rosenberg explains this as the need to "distinguish between what we feel and how we think others react or behave toward us."[49] For example, "I feel unimportant to my coworkers," is an evaluative judgment that describes what one thinks others are thinking and not how that individual feels about him or herself.

Exploring one's feelings and developing a vocabulary for accurately expressing them allows for more honest, open and heartfelt communication. The willingness to be vulnerable with one's feelings in the workplace gives others permission to do the same and is critical to resolving workplace disputes and managing conflicts compassionately and with the highest degree of dignity and respect for all parties. Of utmost importance is that compassionate communication distinguishes the expression of actual feelings from words and statements that convey things other than feelings such as thoughts, assessments and interpretations.[50]

The third step to honest self-expression is taking responsibility for one's feelings and expressing the needs at the root of them. While other people's actions may serve as a catalyst for feelings, all people are responsible for how they choose to receive and experience another person's actions. Every person is the author of his or her own choices. In his seminal book, *Man's Search for Meaning*, psychologist and holocaust survivor Viktor Frankl wrote, "Everything can be taken from a man but one thing: the last of the human freedoms — to choose one's attitude in any given set of circumstances, o choose one's own way."[51] Rosenberg outlines four ways in which people can choose to respond to the negative messages received from others:[52]

1. **Blame one's self.** To blame oneself is to receive the negative message and accept the judgment as accurate and assume responsibility for it. Assuming another person's judgment to be accurate can cause great damage to one's self-esteem.

2. **Blame others.** Rather than assume responsibility for the speaker's negative judgment, this option blames the speaker. Blaming others is an inherently defensive approach that seeks to find fault with the speaker and assumes no responsibility for how one's actions may have played a role in that opinion — regardless of how evaluative it may or may not be. This approach tends to create feelings of anger.

3. **Sense one's own feelings and needs.** This option requires self-reflection in order to gauge one's own feelings and explore the needs that may be creating them. This approach helps achieve clarity about one's underlying needs and can help to surface ideas about how to satisfy those needs.

4. **Sense others' feelings and needs.** This option requires reflecting on the feelings and needs of the speaker in order to gauge that person's feelings and explore the needs that may be creating them. This approach helps achieve clarity about the underlying needs of the speaker and can help to surface ideas about how to satisfy those needs.

Compassionate communication requires that one accept responsibility for his or her feelings by acknowledging the needs, desires and expectations that are at the root of them. One has the greatest chance of having one's needs met when those needs are expressed with vulnerability — openly and honestly.

The fourth step to honest self-expression is to request action to help fulfill one's needs, desires and/or expectations. When making a request to have a need met, use positive action language. This means asking for what is desired rather than what is not desired. For example, a corporate CEO became frustrated because he believed employees were not paying attention to his presentation during a meeting because they were on their computers. He had overheard that some people were multitasking — emailing and conducting other work-related business. At the next company meeting, he asked his assistant to send out a companywide email informing everyone that the meeting was a "no technology meeting." This created much dissatisfaction and conflict because many people used their computers for taking notes. They felt this rule actually inhibited their ability to pay attention and participate in a way that best met their learning needs. What the CEO actually wanted was full participation. But what he asked for prohibited some people from doing so.

Positive action language uses affirming language that inspires others to meet the need with understanding and compassion. The CEO may have received more active participation, which was his goal, had he made the following request: "I have a lot of important information to share with you at our company meeting. Please come to the meeting attentive, focused and prepared to receive this information in whatever way best meets your learning style." The first request inspired anger, aggression and lack of participation; the second request utilizes clear, positive and concrete action language and would most likely have inspired cooperation and compassion.

Positive action language may not always be enough. The person requesting the need has a responsibility to ensure the request is accurately received. Oftentimes a person will make a request by expressing his or her feelings. For example, "I am feeling frustrated that you left the conference room in disarray. Now we have to meet in a disorderly room." Embedded in that "feeling statement" may or may not be a request for the person to clean up the conference right now. If the speaker assumes the request is obvious, but the receiver of the message did not hear a request, conflict ensues. Expressing feelings along with a specific request for action is more likely to result in the need being met. For example, "I am feeling frustrated that you left the conference room in disarray. Can you please clean it up now?" The feeling is expressed and accompanied by a concrete request. Now the receiver of the message has an opportunity to express empathy and meet the underlying need.

Alternatively, a request may sound like a demand if it is not accompanied by the speaker's feelings and needs. For example, "The conference room stinks to high heaven!" The person sending this message may be assuming the receiver of the message will remember that he or she was supposed to clean the conference room, forgot to do so, but is being asked to do it right now. However, without the feeling statement and the specific request for action, this "request to have a need met" is likely to cause confusion, frustration and possibly serve as the catalyst to conflict.

The clearer a request is, the more likely it is to be positively addressed. To ensure a request has been accurately understood, the speaker may want to ask the receiver of the message to reflect back what was asked. Sometimes simply asking, "Does that make sense?" is enough to determine if the message was accurately received. But usually, a more detailed answer is necessary to gain clarity regarding whether or not the receiver understood the entirety of a request. The following questions can help to determine if the receiver of the request fully understood what was being asked:

- Do you mind reflecting back to me what I requested of you?
- Can you summarize for me what we discussed?
- For clarity, do you mind repeating back to me what I asked? I want to make sure I communicated effectively. Can you tell me what you heard me ask?

These questions create opportunities for ensuring the request was accurately understood and for providing additional information if necessary. Collaboration and goodwill can be instilled by providing an affirming statement of appreciation as well as additional clarifying statements to the listener while assuming responsibility for any confusion or lack of clarity. The goal is to engender collaboration. Graciousness goes a long way to accomplishing that.

The following is an example of what honest self-expression might look like in action. *Last month you were late to work 15 times* (observation). *When you are late, I feel resentful because your absence causes me extra work, and I also fear others will grow resentful of you which will impact the morale of the team* (feeling). *I need to be valued in the workplace and to know my contributions are positively experienced. I also need to ensure I am fostering an environment where others can experience that as well* (needs). *Can you help me understand why you are frequently late so that we can develop a plan to work together in a way that meets both our needs* (request)? *I want to make sure I am communicating effectively. Do you mind reflecting back to me what I just expressed* (request for reflection)? *Thank you. I can see you understand me, and I appreciate your willingness to work together in creating a more positive working relationship* (expressing appreciation).

A final note regarding the process of honest self-expression: Seek out honest feedback from the listener. Collaboration — the action of working with someone to produce or create something — is by definition a shared experience. Bringing the listener, or receiver of messages, into the process by requesting feedback deepens the collaboration, increases opportunities for growth, enhances opportunities for developing trust and opens doors to new ways of experiencing the relationship with that person. Consider inquiring how the listener is feeling; what the listener is thinking; and whether the listener would be willing to take a particular action. Seeking honesty and requesting honesty is an important aspect of fostering compassionate communication and building peace.

A Framework for Receiving With Empathy

Communication is a process of sending messages (self-expression) and listening (receiving the self-expression of others). Receiving with empathy is hearing what others observe, feel, need and request with a respectful understanding of what they are experiencing. Empathy is the birthplace of human-to-human connectivity and is at the heart of human security. In order to exercise empathy, one must shed all preconceived ideas and judgments about a person and his or her ideas and actions. Approaches to compassionate listening include:

- Keeping an open heart
- Being sincere
- Exercising curiosity
- Exercising patience
- Staying with the person and the problem (i.e., listening as a human being and not as a given role such as boss, employee, co-worker, client, customer, etc.)

Receiving with empathy is listening to understand. No matter what the person may express and no matter what attitude or tone the person may take in order to self-express, compassionate listening is focused only on hearing what the other person observes, feels, needs and requests and doing this without judgment or evaluation.

Empathy calls for extending one's full focus on simply understanding what the other person is experiencing and needing and allowing that person as much time and space as necessary to fully self-express. Being fully present is a kill one must practice and be in constant self-awareness of. n his book *Nonviolent Communication*, Rosenburg notes the ollowing behaviors as indicators that one has slipped out of istening and in to some other behavior that is often mistaken ıs listening:[53]

- **Giving advice** — the listener provides instructions or directions on how to move forward or how to avoid this situation from happening in the future
- **One-upping** — the listener offers examples of how something even worse happened to him or her
- **Educating** — the listener takes the opportunity to provide a teaching moment about how to learn from the problem
- **Consoling** — the listener offers emotional support and assures the person the problem was not his or her fault
- **Storytelling** — the listener offers a "this reminds me of a time" story or an example of how this same problem has been experienced by others
- **Shutting down** — the listener offers words of advise intended to stop the other person from talking such as "cheer up" or "don't feel so bad"
- **Sympathizing** — the listener offers "petting" language such as "oh honey," "bless your heart" or "you poor thing"
- **Interrogating** — the listener take on the role of intelligence gathering in order to secure all the details of the problem
- **Explaining** — the listener provides self-justifying actions regarding the problem such as "I would have called but ..."
- **Correcting** — the listener indicates that the way the speaker experienced the problem was not factually correct

Listening with empathy is not listening for one's own intellectual understanding; rather, it is holding space for that person to fully self-express and giving that person the gift of understanding and compassion for what he or she may be feeling, needing and requesting.

Receiving with empathy is listening for feelings Listening with empathy is listening for what a person feels rather than what a person thinks. For example, a person may say, "I just feel Sally is being really aggressive with me about the deadline. She needs to back off!" What this person thinks is that Sally is being overly demanding. But what this person may feel is scared that she will not meet Sally's expectations and that the team or project will fail because of it. By listening for the feeling behind the "thinking," one is able to begin to get at the root of the conflict.

Receiving with empathy requires paraphrasing. Listening for the feeling behind the thinking requires a bit of guesswork. And that is OK. Paraphrasing helps to uncover whether or not the listener accurately understood and guessed the speaker's feelings. Reflecting back to the speaker what was understood gives the speaker the opportunity to affirm that the listener heard the feeling correctly. If not, it provides the speaker the opportunity to continue to self-express and clarify. Reflecting back to the speaker also provides the added benefit of giving the speaker the experience of reflecting on his or her own self-expression and perhaps delving deeper into the thinking and perspectives expressed.

Paraphrasing can take the form of questions in order to reveal the speaker's understanding as well as to elicit any corrections the speaker may want to offer. For demonstration purposes, the following examples relate to the employee who was habitually late for work and what empathetic listening might look like on his or her part:[54]

1. **Questions that reflect what others are observing** — "Are you reacting to how many meetings I was either late to or failed to attend last week?"

2. **Questions that reflect what others are feeling and the needs behind their feelings** — "Are you feeling scared that my absences will cause the project to fail and you want to ensure you and the team are not blamed for the failure?"

3. **Questions that reflect what others are requesting** — "Are you wanting me to assure you that I will attend the remaining meetings, and that I will work late to make up for lost time so the project is successful?"

These types of paraphrasing questions require a bit of guesswork on the part of the listener in order to engage the process of deeper understanding while inviting corrections for what was not understood accurately and demonstrating authenticity in one's desire to understand.

Paraphrasing is helpful when messages are emotionally charged, the message is complex or the possibility of not understanding is high or is an established precedence in a particular relationship. Paraphrasing could be perceived as condescending if it is unnecessary. Therefore, only paraphrase when doing so contributes to increased compassion and a deepening of understanding.

Receiving with empathy seeks to understand and honor the feelings and needs the speaker is experiencing and is a process of discovering the request the speaker may have even when that person does not have the communication acumen to pointedly make the request. Compassionate communication is life affirming and, therefore, does not condemn or punish a speaker who does not have the skills to communicate effectively, efficiently or compassionately. Receiving with empathy teaches compassion by modeling it one interaction at a time.

Active Listening

Active listening is a method of listening and responding attentively with the intent of building rapport and trust while deepening one's understanding of the other person. The goal of active listening is to deepen one's connection to the person with whom communication is occurring and to gain a richer understanding of the speaker's feelings and needs and to begin to "hear" a request even when one is not directly spoken. The following is a list of active listening skills that can be incorporated as needed in the process of empathetic receiving.

- **Acknowledging:** Acknowledging statements are designed to recognize and name the emotions, feelings and intentions of the speaker. Examples of acknowledging statements include, "I can see this situation scares you. Can you help me understand more about the fear you are feeling?" or "I can understand why you may feel anxious. I would like to know more about why this situation is creating anxiety for you." Acknowledging invites deeper exploration of feelings and helps the speaker and listener to connect to the need that is driving the feeling. Acknowledging may require some initial guessing in order to accurately name the emotion. Be sensitive to how the other person will experience this form of active listening and ensure the labeling is presented in such a way that engages the speaker rather than puts him or her on the defense.

- **Clarifying**: Clarifying questions help the speaker more fully explain the points being made and demonstrate that the listener is paying attention and is curious about the content of the speaker's message. Clarifying questions focus on facts rather than emotions and can help to de-escalate the speaker if he or she has become emotionally hijacked or is verging on an emotional hijack. Examples of clarifying questions include, "When did this happen?" "Can you recall additional details?" "How did others respond to the situation?" "What else happened?"

- **Encouraging:** Encouraging comments and questions create opportunities for the speaker to share his or her feelings and needs, demonstrating to the person that how he or she feels is important and valued. Examples include, "Please tell me more;" "Help me understand;" and "How did that make you feel?"

- **Mirroring:** Mirroring is a method of engaging mirror

neurons by reflecting back to the speaker his or her emotions, feelings, body language, tone of voice, etc., to demonstrate a shared experience in the communication rather than a disinterested observer. If the speaker assumes a defensive or aggressive posture, the listener can assume one as well and then move to a more open one in order to begin to create a shift in the energy of the communication.

- **Normalizing:** Normalizing helps the speaker to feel that his or her feelings are appropriate to the situation. Normalizing statements may include, "Considering what you have experienced in the past, this is an appropriate way to be feeling right now." Or, "This is a normal way to feel after something like this." Normalizing helps the person to feel safe expressing difficult emotions and to muster the courage to be vulnerable when sharing difficult thoughts and feelings.

- **Reframing:** Reframing the speaker's message preserves the meta message contained within the content while rewording its expression. This allows the message to be framed in positive action language that moves toward an understanding of the need hidden within the feelings.

- **Summarizing:** Summarizing helps the speaker to be understood. By repeating back to the speaker what was heard and understood demonstrates that the listener is paying attention and has a desire to understand the speaker. It also provides an opportunity for the speaker to clarify or correct anything the listener did not understand correctly.

- **Supplementing:** Supplementing is a form of active listening that uses "and" in place of "but." For example, rather than saying "yes, but ..." saying "yes, and ..." changes the message from potentially putting the listener on defensive to encouraging collaboration from the listener.

- **Validating:** Validating honors the speaker's contributions to the communication and demonstrates appreciation for the person's thoughts, feelings, needs and requests. When validating, try to mention specific points the speaker contributed to the communication. Examples of validating may include, "Thank you for your willingness to speak with me about this issue. I really value your input;" or, "I know it took courage to share your thoughts and feelings with me. Thank you for doing so. I really learned a lot."

Active listening techniques are valuable to the process of compassionate communication in that these skills can help to deepen the human-to-human connection as one receives empathically and seeks to understand the observations, feelings, need and requests of the speaker.

CHAPTER THREE

WAR IN THE WORKPLACE

DEALING WITH BULLYING BEHAVIOR AND
OPPRESSIVE PERSONALITIES

*Acceptance, appreciation and experiencing one's contributions to a group in a positive way
all foster human-to-human connectivity and help a person to feel validated
and confirmed in his or her sense of self.*

THE PREFACE OF THIS BOOK listed the four human rights, as outlined by the "Universal Declaration of Human Rights," that relate to the workplace that are inherent to all people. The rights are as follows:

1. Everyone has the right to work, to free choice of employment, to just and favorable conditions of work and to protection against unemployment.
2. Everyone, without any discrimination, has the right to equal pay for equal work.
3. Everyone who works has the right to just and favorable remuneration ensuring for himself and his family an existence worthy of human dignity, and supplemented, if necessary, by other means of social protection.
4. Everyone has the right to form and to join trade unions for the protection of his interests.

Individuals who wage war in the workplace through bullying behavior frequently violate these human rights, causing great harm to the individual(s) with whom their wars are waged as well as the organization itself. Bullying behavior is extraordinarily common. A study conducted by Workplace Bullying Institute found that 65.6 million people have been affected by bullying behavior in the workplace. Additional findings include:[55]

- 27 percent of workers have direct experience with abusive conduct at work
- 56 percent of bullying behavior is by managers, supervisors and people in leadership positions
- Men are more likely than women to demonstrate bullying behavior (69 percent versus 31 percent), but women target other women at a higher rate than men do (68 percent versus 57 percent)
- Men and women alike target women at a higher rate than they target men
- 72 percent of employers deny, discount, encourage, rationalize or defend bullying in the workplace

The institute defines bullying behavior as "repeated mistreatment; abusive conduct that is: threatening, humiliating or intimidating, work sabotage or verbal abuse."[56] Ralph H. Kilmann, co-author of the Thomas-Kilmann Conflict Mode Instrument, describes individuals who demonstrate bullying behavior as people who make "life in the organization unbearable, dangerous and fearful for others — usually by their extreme aggressiveness and sometimes by their extreme passivity."[57]

The Workplace Bullying Institute study also found that employers frequently fail to appropriately react to abusive conduct and are far more likely to deny the behavior is occurring or discount the impact of it, leading to 61 percent of targets leaving their jobs as the only way to eliminate the bullying. Rather than taking positive actions to stop the bullying behavior and support the person who is being harmed by it, employers tend to create additional harm.[58]

- 25 percent of employers deny bullying behavior exists
- 16 percent of employers discount the behavior
- 15 percent rationalize it
- 12 percent eliminate the behavior in some manner
- 11 percent defend it
- 10 percent acknowledge it but fail to address it
- 6 percent condemn it
- 5 percent encourage it

RECOGNIZING WORKPLACE BULLYING

There are subtle and not so subtle behaviors indicative of bullying. The following 20 signs can be difficult to detect until patterns are well established, which can takes months or years. Yet, the anxiety and emotional upset they cause are felt each time the behavior is presented.[59]

1. **Deceit:** Repeatedly lying; creating false hopes with no plans to fulfill them

2. **Intimidation:** Using fear-inducing language and behavior

3. **Ignoring:** Failing to invite someone to a meeting; purposefully avoiding the person or being selective in the attention that is paid

4. **Isolation/exclusion:** Excluding someone intentionally or making them feel socially or physically isolated from a group, as well as excluding individuals from decisions, conversations and work-related events

5. **Rationalization:** Constantly justifying or defending bullying behavior

6. **Minimization:** Discounting or failing to address someone's legitimate concerns or feelings

7. **Diversion:** Dodging issues, acting oblivious or changing the subject to distract away from particular issues (i.e., canceling or no-showing meetings and avoiding people)

8. **Shame and guilt:** Making an individual constantly feel that they are the problem; shaming them for no real wrongdoing or making them feel inadequate and unworthy

9. **Undermining work:** Deliberately delaying and/or blocking an individual's work; repeated betrayal; promising projects and then giving them to others; alternating supportive and undermining behavior

10. **Pitting employees against each other:** Attempting to drive competition by pitting employees against one another; establishing a "winners and losers" culture; encouraging employees to turn against one another

11. **Removal of responsibility:** Removing someone's responsibilities; changing his or her role; or replacing aspects of his job without cause

12. **Impossible or changing expectations:** Not establishing a job description or key areas of responsibilities; setting nearly impossible expectations and work guidelines; changing those expectations frequently so employees cannot be successful

13. **Constant change and inconsistency:** Constantly changing expectations, guidelines and scope of assignments; inconsistency of word and action

14. **Mood swings:** Sharp and sudden shifts in emotions

15. **Criticism:** Constantly criticizing someone's work or behavior

16. **Withholding information:** Intentionally withholding information from someone or giving them the wrong information

17. **Projection of blame:** Shifting blame to others and using them as a scapegoat

18. **Taking credit:** Taking credit for other people's ideas and contributions without acknowledging them

19. **Seduction:** Using excessive flattery and compliments to gain trust and lower defenses so the person is more responsive to manipulative behavior

20. **Creating a feeling of uselessness:** Making an individual feel underused; rarely communicating with the employee about his or her work; persistently giving employees unfavorable duties and responsibilities

The following bullying behaviors are far more overt and easily recognizable:

1. **Aggression:** Yelling or shouting at an individual, exhibiting aggression verbally or nonverbally (e.g. pounding a desk, ripping up work)

2. **Intrusion:** Intruding on someone by lurking around his or her desk

3. **Coercion:** Aggressively persuading someone to say or do something against his or her better judgment

4. **Punishment:** Punishing an individual psychologically through passive aggression or emotionally through isolation

5. **Belittling:** Disparaging someone or their opinions, ideas, work or personal circumstances in an undeserving manner

6. **Embarrassment:** Degrading or humiliating an individual in front of others

7. **Revenge:** Seeking unfair revenge when a mistake happens; retaliating against an employee

8. **Threats:** Threatening unwarranted punishment, discipline, termination and/or emotional or psychological abuse

9. **Campaigning:** Launching an overt or underhanded campaign to diminish a person in hopes of forcing them to leave the job or the organization

10. **Blocking advancement or growth:** Impeding an individual's progression, growth and/or advancement in the organization unfairly

IMPACTS OF BULLYING

Although bullying behavior can often be the catalyst of short-term spikes in production, the behavior is insidious to creating long-term productivity. A study conducted by Dr. John J. Medina, a developmental molecular biologist who is an affiliate professor of Bioengineering at the University of Washington School of Medicine, found that individuals who are bullied in the workplace performed 50 percent worse on cognitive tests than their non-bullied counterparts. Another study conducted by Dr. Noreen Tehrani, a psychologist with expertise in trauma, found that individuals who experience workplace bullying exhibit similar psychological and physical symptoms — such as nightmares and anxiety — as victims of violence from Northern Ireland and soldiers returning from overseas combat. Another study conducted by Anna Nyberg of the Stress Institute in Stockholm of more than 3,100 men in a typical workplace environment over the course of a 10-year period found that employees with bullying supervisors — defined as incompetent, inconsiderate, secretive and uncommunicative — were 60 percent more likely to suffer a heart attack or other life-threatening heart conditions. Bullying behavior creates a ripple effect of negative consequences on a person's physical, mental and economic well-being as well as having negative impacts on co-worker relationships and relationships with friends and family.

How Bullying Affects the Brain and Body

Stress is the biological human response to on-going mental and emotional strains. Low-level stress can be an important catalyst to action and change, but when stress is significant and enduring, the physical consequences can be severe. Long periods of exposure to workplace bullying can have a profound impact on a person's physical health. Individuals who bully others create a notable amount of stress for a person, as do the coworkers and supervisors who stand by and do nothing about it, especially when it is the person's job to do something (i.e., human resources, direct supervisors or senior management). Exposure to distressing situations triggers the automatically coordinated release of glucocorticoids, including the hormone cortisol. These hormones flood the brain and body, which can, over a prolonged period of time, cause atrophy of areas of the brain responsible for memory, emotional regulation and the ability to sustain positive social relationships.

Prolonged exposure to highly stressful workplace conflict can lead to the following stress-related diseases and health complications:[60]

- Cardiovascular issues, such as high blood pressure, stroke and heart attack
- Adverse neurological changes such as neurotransmitter disruption, hippocampus and amygdala atrophy
- Gastrointestinal disorders such as IBD and colitis
- Immunological impairment
- Auto-immune disorders
- Fibromyalgia and chronic fatigue syndrome
- Diabetes
- Skin disorders

The following are symptoms that may be indicative of the above stress:

- Nausea
- Tremors of the lips, hands, etc.
- Feeling uncoordinated
- Chills
- Profuse sweating
- Diarrhea
- Rapid heartbeat
- Rapid breathing
- Elevated blood pressure
- Chest pain
- Uncontrollable crying
- Headaches

Psychological and Emotional Effects of Bullying

Bullying behavior is a form of psychological harassment and violence because it affects a person's mental health and sense of well-being. The targeted and highly personalized nature of bullying has a profound impact on a person's identity, ego strength and ability to rebound from the assaults. Prolonged exposure to bullying can compromise both the target's physical and mental health. Some of the psychological effects include:

- Debilitating anxiety
- Panic attacks
- Clinical depression

- Post-traumatic stress (PTSD)
- Shame
- Guilt
- Overwhelming sense of injustice

Post-traumatic stress is a serious consequence of bullying and can develop when a person experiences highly traumatizing environments that exhaust his or her natural coping mechanisms, which includes working conditions void of control and predictability. The effects of trauma can last long after the exposure to the trauma.

Social Effects of Bullying

The human brain is wired for connectivity, which means that all humans desire meaningful relationships with others. Acceptance, appreciation and experiencing one's contributions to a group in a positive way all foster human-to-human connectivity and help one to feel validated and confirmed in his or her sense of self. Kipling Williams, professor of psychology in the department of psychological sciences at Purdue University and expert on ostracism, explains in an *Annual Review of Psychology* article[61] that when an individual is ostracized — defined as "ignoring and excluding individuals or groups by individuals or groups" — that being ignored, excluded, and/or rejected creates a form of pain and distress that is both reflexive and adaptive for survival. Brief exposures to ostracism can result in sadness and anger, causing individuals to seek to overcome those feelings in several ways: 1) by attempting to fortify relational needs (e.g., belonging, self-esteem, shared understanding and trust) via prosocial thoughts and behaviors; or 2) by attempting to fortify self-efficacy and existence needs such as control and recognition via anti-social thoughts and behaviors. However, chronic exposure to ostracism can deplete coping resources, causing depression and a sense of helplessness.[62]

One study found that groups have a tendency to reject group members whose generosity exceeds the generosity of the average group member or most powerful member(s) of the group. Altruism, in the face of greed and self-interest, is difficult to tolerate because it creates discomfort for those who are less generous. The less generous among the group also fear the altruist will muck up the group's norm by pushing it to be better than it actually is, and resent the minority membership for pushing the group toward a higher ethical standard than what the average group member (or most powerful group member) wants for the group. This shunning can be painful, and can challenge the prosocial assumptions about the world the bullied person may hold.[63]

Economic Effects of Bullying

Workplace bullying inherently affects a person's sense of safety. When bullying occurs in the workplace, the target of bullying is challenged to feel confident that his or her livelihood is assured, which may be precisely what the person demonstrating the bullying behavior hopes to achieve. When a person assumes control over a person's livelihood through bullying behavior — which occurs in 72 percent of workplace bullying situations, he or she has significant leverage to cause financial pain. Understandably, single parent workers are the most vulnerable to being bullied.

When a person in leadership or management implements bullying behavior, that person can block transfers to a safe job and/or make the bullied person feel so miserable that he or she ultimately resigns. The behavior can cause so much stress that it affects the bullied person's health severely forcing him or her to resign in order to cease and recover from the stress. This is termed "constructive discharge." A 2010 Workplace Bullying Institute survey found that 13 percent of individuals who experienced workplace bullying were forced to transfer from a job they loved to another position within the organization in order to stop the bullying; 24 percent were constructively discharged from employment; and 40 percent resigned their jobs in order to reverse declining physical and mental health.[64]

Effects of Bullying on Family Life

Most people spend more time with their coworkers than they do their families, which means when there is trouble at work, that trouble inevitably follows a person home. When an individual is being targeted with bullying behavior in the workplace, it has a direct impact on his or her family. Home is often the only safe outlet for frustrations and anger, but if misplaced, the expression of anger and frustration can cause harm to loved ones and damage family relationships. In an effort to not misdirect negative emotions toward loved ones, individuals experiencing bullying in the workplace may choose to emotionally withdraw instead. Rather than spew pent up, negative emotions on to loved ones, they withdraw from the family, choosing to remain silent rather than expose the people they care the most about to the negativity. The inability to effectively manage the emotions and access the support necessary to process them in a healthy manner can lead to loss of sleep, loss of appetite (or an increase appetite in the form of emotional eating), an increase in alcohol consumption and other unhealthy forms of coping that can cause a person to neglect his or her family.

Effects of Bullying on Co-worker Relationships

A Workplace Bullying Institute survey found that less than 1 percent of bullying cases result in coworkers joining together to confront superiors about the situation. Almost always, workplace bullying results in coworkers alienating the bullied individual, and worse, the targeted person is often condemned by coworkers for not standing up for him or herself. Coworkers often believe that had they been the targets of abuse they would have done something to stop it. This belief that if presented with a similar situation the person would handle things differently is due to optimism bias (also known as unrealistic or comparative optimism), which is a cognitive bias that causes a person to believe that he or she is less at risk of experiencing a negative event compared to others. This belief that a person would innately have the knowledge, skills and courage to handle a situation in a more positive and self-protecting manner leads to the condemnation of the person who did not. And this condemnation leads to blame, shame, alienation and justification that the targeted person likely got exactly what he or she deserves. In essence, optimization bias leads coworkers to retaliate against the victim, perpetuating, prolonging and exacerbating the targeted person's suffering.

Social inclusion is a fundamental human need, and when coworkers fail to support the person who is being targeted, and worse yet, condemn and alienate the person, not only is this human need not being met but the basic human right to experience "just and favorable conditions of work" is also denied. This creates a work environment plagued with fear, insecurity and unhappiness. And with prolonged exposure to condemnation and alienation, people begin to become traumatized and depressed. Symptoms of trauma include:[65]

- Intrusive, negative or fearful thoughts that interfere with normal cognition
- Flashbacks and replaying of horrific incidents invade routine days and nights
- A sense of apprehension over future negative events leads traumatized individuals to lash out at others
- Avoiding locations, tasks and people who are reminders of traumatizing incidents

Individuals who demonstrate bullying behavior are the sources of work trauma. And unlike PTSD that originates from surviving natural disasters and accidents, bullying is intentional and highly targeted.

TARGETS OF BULLYING BEHAVIOR

People who experience workplace bullying most often represent a *perceived* threat to the person who is displaying bullying behavior. This threat may be seem apparent to the person or it may be experienced by the person at an unconscious level — meaning the threat may be only perception and not an actual, intentional act of aggression on the part of the target. The perception of threat is based on how a person feels in response to the targeted individual's words and/or actions and may have more to do with previous experiences of the person who is demonstrating bullying behavior, past experiences of rejection or failure, fear of being perceived as weak or incompetent or a host of other reasons that are about the perpetrator of bullying rather than about the target of the bullying behavior.

Years of research conducted by Workplace Bullying Institute have uncovered several common characteristics held by individuals who are most likely to experience bullying in the workplace. Individuals who experience workplace bullying tend to be veteran professionals and/or the most skilled individuals in the work group. They are likely to be independent, highly capable people who are not subservient, and therefore may intentionally or unintentionally challenge the status quo. They are often the person others turn to for guidance, due to their high emotional intelligence, social skills and empathic way of communicating and relating. They tend to be ethical and honest people who are conscientious of doing the "right thing." Consequently, they are often whistleblowers. According to Workplace Bullying Institute, "The most easily exploited targets are people with personalities founded on a prosocial orientation — a desire to help, heal, teach, develop and nurture others." Targets of bullying are likely to be non-confrontational and unlikely to respond to aggression with aggression.[66]

USING COMPASSIONATE COMMUNICATION

In his book, *The Third Side*, author William Ury makes the claim that "Whatever the surface issues in dispute, the underlying cause of conflict usually lies in the deprivation of basic human needs like love and respect. Frustration leads people to bully others, to use violence, and to grab someone else's things." He goes on to claim that all people want to feel "safe, respected and free."[67]

The basic human needs are quite simple, and yet there is a human tendency to over complicate the process of getting needs met in a manner that is fair, equitable and just. Utilizing the four stages of compassionate communication — 1) observing without evaluation; 2) identifying the feelings being expressed; 3) uncovering the need at the root of the feeling(s); and 4) making a request — the person being bullied as well as the person who might otherwise default to bullying can begin to understand that the needs of all parties on all sides of a conflict most likely share the same goals: to feel safe, respected and free. Once commonality is established, the parties can understand that while there may be a lot of work that goes into arriving at a peaceable agreement, they are much more similar in their needs than they are different.

TACTICS FOR IN-THE-MOMENT SELF-CARE

Individuals who default to bullying behavior do so most often because they have not learned prosocial ways in which to get their needs meet. Whether it is accurate or not, they often feel as under attack as the person at whom their bullying behavior s targeted. This feeling of attack can cause an emotional hijack, also known as an amygdala hijack (see Chapter 1). When a person is hijacked inappropriately (i.e., when that person's life is truly not in danger), there are techniques for engaging the prefrontal cortex and fostering cognition to inform productive behavior. The following techniques are interventions for a person who often defaults to bullying behavior and/or the person who is experiencing bullying to disengage the amygdala and re-engage the prefrontal cortex:[68]

- **Breathe**: Oxygen increases the blood flow to the brain. It also engages the prefrontal cortex.
- **Write**: Whether writing in a journal or simply grabbing a piece of paper and initiating the process of writing, this activity requires the engagement of the prefrontal cortex.
- **Get curious**: Observe the "facts on the street" without evaluation. Describe exactly what is happening. What can be recognized (seen, heard, smelled) and labeled. Curiosity is a function of the prefrontal cortex.
- **Label feelings**: Recognize the feeling that is being experienced, and give it a name. The moment a person recognizes the feeling, it creates a shift that begins to disengage the amygdala and engage the prefrontal cortex.
- **Think positive**. Provide self-care and extend care to the other person by silently chanting "compassion, compassion, compassion," until a shift in the mind and body is experienced. By focusing on compassion rather than fear, the body will begin to elicit the "tend and

befriend" hormone oxytocin, which will automatically allow feelings of compassion and tenderness to replace feelings of fear, pain or anger.

- **Change locations**: Removing one's self from the environment that is causing the amygdala to become activated allows the brain the space to process what occurred and to apply cognitive thinking to the situation that may help the individual reframe the situation.

Eliminating workplace bullying and implementing processes, procedures and conflict resolution practices to ensure employees at every level of the company have the ability to manage conflict effectively and productively while also ensuring justice and human dignity for all parties is paramount to fostering a collaborative and high-performing work environment. This requires an intentional effort on the part of the c-suite and senior leadership to implement and champion conflict management and peace-building practices that place honesty, empathy and integrity as the cornerstones of corporate culture and business practices. Peace in the workplace is a day-by-day journey that requires an unwavering commitment to holding human security and dignity as the highest business priority.

CHAPTER FOUR

DIFFERENCES IN THE WORKPLACE
GENDER, CULTURE AND CONFLICT

Workplace diversity offers numerous benefits to organizations, employees and customers, and it is also a human right.

THERE HAS NEVER BEEN A time in human history in which working with, appreciating and understanding differences has been more important — both personally and professionally. The world is getting smaller and smaller as technology continues to shape how, when and where work is done, creating the possibility to interact with employees, clients and business partners anywhere in the world at any time. Businesses are becoming increasingly globalized, and with that globalization comes numerous benefits and challenges. This movement toward globalization is precisely why organizations should seek to embrace diversity in the workplace and value the differences diversity brings to organizations.

Diversity is a general term that refers to the variety of differences among people in an organization such as race, ethnic group, gender, sexual orientation, age, personality, cognitive style, tenure within the organization and/or within one's selected field, organizational role and function, education, background and more. Diversity includes not only how others perceive an individual but also how individuals perceive themselves, because these external and internal perceptions influence interactions. For a diverse group of employees to work productively and peacefully together, intentional efforts toward effective communication, adaptability and change must be implemented and embraced.

BENEFITS OF DIFFERENCES IN THE WORKPLACE

Decades of research indisputably demonstrate that workplace diversity enhances decision-making, problem-solving, creativity, innovation and flexibility. Organizations that actively assess strategies for embracing differences in the workplace and develop and implement diversity plans experience the following benefits.

- **Increased adaptability**: Diverse organizations are able to leverage an enhanced variety of solutions to challenges in services, sourcing and allocation of resources because the individual contributors are able to draw from a variety of different backgrounds. This diversity allows for the unique talents and experiences to shape ideating for solutions that are flexible and agile to fluctuations in the marketplace as well as customer demands.
- **Enhanced range of services**: With a diverse array of skills, experiences and perspectives paired with a range of languages and cultural understandings, companies can more effectively and authentically operate in a global market.
- **Multiple viewpoints**: When diverse organizations foster a culture in which differences are embraced, the organization, employees and customers all benefit

from a pool of ideas that have been developed from unique experiences and perspectives. This diverse pool of ideas allows for more creative, innovative and effective approaches to meeting the needs of business strategies, organizational challenges and customers.

- **More effective execution**: Diversity inspires high performance, which ultimately results in higher productivity, profit and return on investments.

While workplace diversity offers numerous benefits to organizations, employees and customers, it is also a human right. Considering the fact that the "Universal Declaration of Human Rights" asserts that all people have the right to work, to free choice of employment, to just and favorable conditions without any discrimination and with equal pay for equal work, organizations have a responsibility to foster workplace cultures that welcome and embrace differences.

CHALLENGES ASSOCIATED WITH DIVERSITY IN THE WORKPLACE

Managing differences may be beneficial, but it is not without its challenges. Personality clashes, lack of curiosity, lack of cultural understanding, variances in communication style and protocols as it relates to cultural norms, power and authority and a host of other issues can all present barriers to experiencing the benefits associated with workplace diversity. Following is an overview of challenges organizations might experience when differences exist in the workplace without a strategy for embracing them.

- **Communication planning**: Perceptual, cultural and language differences must be understood and embraced in order to experience the benefits of diversity in the workplace. That means diversity training is necessary to provide insights into the myriad social and professional norms that influence perceptions, expectations and performance. In addition to diversity training, a communication plan that highlights key issues relevant to an organization's unique set of workplace differences should be implemented to ensure the diversity training remains both relevant and actionable.

- **Change management**: Resistance to change is normal and should be expected. Every organization includes individuals who are particularly resistant to change. Implementing a change management program designed to overcome the "we've always done it this way" mentality is critical to the emergence of new ideas and to fostering a progressive and innovative culture in which curiosity trumps complacency.

- **Workplace diversity policy implementation and ongoing management**: To be successful, diversity policy implementation must be a top-down strategy. Buy-in from the c-suite and executive leadership is paramount to success. In addition to executive buy-in, creating a committee that is responsible for implementing the policy as well as coming up with new ideas for both attracting and incorporating more diversity to the company will help to further integrate a culture of diversity within the organization. The organization's mission, vision and values may need to be amended in order to bring authenticity to the effort. (Learn more about creating vision, mission and values in Chapter 5).

Assessing the effectiveness and success of a workplace diversity policy and plan requires engagement with the workforce on a consistent basis. Many organizations utilize employee satisfaction surveys, which serve several beneficial purposes.

- Surveys demonstrate to employees that the organization is about action rather than words.
- Surveying employees keeps management and senior leadership in tune with the realities of the workplace and surfaces areas where challenges and obstacles may be present, as well as which policies need to be revised or eliminated.
- Surveying employees provides a means for measuring effectiveness.

Organizations that are truly committed to embracing the benefits of differences in the workplace and fostering a culture where diversity is celebrated will demonstrate this in hiring practices at every level of the organization — from the c-suite to midlevel management to production and front line employees.

UNDERSTANDING CULTURE

Culture is comprised of values, norms and beliefs. When considering culture from the perspective of workplace diversity, this concept relates to the values, norms and beliefs of the individual employees or members of an organization. However, every organization has its own culture that exists in tandem with the cultures of the employees and / or members. From an organizational perspective, culture is the collective values, norms and beliefs that represent how an organization wants to be experienced in the marketplace, as well as how it wants to be experienced by customers, potential customers and employees. Culture is shared; it is intangible; it is learned and dynamic; and it influences how the world is perceived.[69] This holds true for the cultures of the individuals who make up the employees or members of an organization as well as for the organization itself. An important element of developing a diversity strategy, as well as developing an organization's vision, mission and values are to consider how the cultures of the individuals *within* the organization and the culture *of* the organization support and complement one another. The most well-thought out organizational culture will fail if the cultures of those individuals within the organization clash with it.

All cultures, whether individual or organizational, operate under a set of fundamental assumptions. If these assumptions are not brought to the surface through dialogue and open exchanges of self-expression, they can become catalysts for conflict. Recognizing that "you don't know what you don't know" is paramount to unearthing the assumptions that exist within an organization and bringing them to conscious awareness so they can be acknowledged and an opportunity for learning can be made available. This chapter explores the aspects of culture that easily fall into the "assumption trap."

Types of Communication

There are four primary types of communication that affect culture and that, when understood and practiced effectively, can reduce conflict and enhance peace in the workplace.

1. High versus low context
2. Verbal communication
3. Non-verbal communications
4. Listening

High Versus Low Context

Certain cultures assume that knowledge of a situation and the appropriate way to behave in a situation are acquired through built-in expectations of what is customary and ordinary within that culture. There is little use for formalized agreements or lengthy discussions to decide what is appropriate in a given situation — the parties are assumed to have acquired this knowledge from experience. This is considered to be a "high context" culture. A "low context" culture is a culture in which information and rules are abundant and clearly stated. There is a general focus on rules and people assume the *literal meaning*s of words are the *intended meaning*s of words. In a high context culture, rules are implicit, which means dealing with parties from high context cultures can present challenges for those who identify with a low context culture. For example, Japanese people traditionally expect others in a negotiation to sense the context and act in an expected manner. An inexperienced negotiator may overly belabor a point in the eyes of the Japanese parties while the low-context negotiator may feel he or she is only fully exploring options. Active listening is a crucial skill in working with people from high-context cultures, as the listener must look beyond what is stated. The table below demonstrates how high and low contexts differ.

HIGH CONTEXT: IMPLICIT/INDIRECT	LOW CONTEXT: EXPLICIT/DIRECT
• Knowledge is acquired through a built in expectation of what is customary within a culture.	• Information and rules are abundant and clearly stated. There is a focus on rules and the literal meanings of words.
• Non-verbal messages and gestures are important.	• Statements are taken at face value, and there is little about the process that is assumed.
• Saving face and tact are important.	• Expectations are discussed.
• Rules are implicit.	• Direct questions are not meant to offend.
• There is little use for formalized agreements, the parties "know" from experience.	• Indirect cues may be ineffectual.

Adapted from intractablitly.org and Edward Hall, Hidden *Dimensions of Time* and Dodd, C.H, *Dynamics of Intercultural Communication*

Individuals who identify with high context cultures tend to be diplomatic, face-saving and non-confrontational people who experience a shared history and culture. High context cultures often communicate in a high context manner and easily understand one another when doing so. High context cultures are very relationally focused, and while many assumptions are made, they are not experienced as assumptions but rather rely on the listener to intuit the meaning. In contrast, low context cultures expect and rely on very clear communication and clear accountability. Low context cultures demonstrate power and assertiveness in order to gets things done. This can be perceived as rude and dominating to individuals from high context cultures. In general, the United States is a more direct, low context country, while Japan is one of the least direct cultures. Examples of high context cultures are Japan, China, Indonesia, India, Southeast Asian countries and the Native American Indian culture. Examples of midrange context cultures are Middle Eastern countries, African countries and Latin American countries. Examples of low context countries include Northern and Eastern European countries, the United States and Canada.

Within the context of high and low cultures, there is also the element of high and low individualism. Individualism is a social theory that favors freedom of action or individuals over collective control. Individualistic cultures tend to be:

- Independent
- Self-directed
- Assume responsibility for self
- Competitive
- Self-focused (i.e., responsible for self, self-motivated, high achievers, etc.)
- Motivated by recognition

Individualistic cultures assume allegiance to self rather than to the group.

In contrast, collective cultures are group oriented, and allegiance is given to the group rather than to self. Collective cultures value community and an individual's own sense of self is in relationship to who he or she is within the community and that person's relationships with other people. Therefore, within a collective culture, individual decision-making is influenced by how one person's decisions may affect the community, including one's own family. Collective cultures can be either lineal collective or collateral collectives. Lineal collectives experience themselves in relationship to their lineage (i.e., Jewish, Irish, African-American, etc.); collateral collectives experience themselves as a formation of a group for a particular purpose (i.e., educational class, training program, degree program). Nuclear families are often collateral formations. Organizational structures such as businesses or churches are often collateral formations. The following table demonstrates the difference between individualistic and collectivist cultures.

INDIVIDUALISTIC	COLLECTIVISTIC
• People are independent and autonomous.	• People are part of a circle of relationships.
• Identity is individual.	• Identity is as a member of a group.
• In conflict, response is individual.	• In conflict, response is chosen jointly.
• Achievement involves individual goal-setting and action.	• Maintaining group harmony is important.
• Everyone is capable of making is or her own choices.	• Choices are made in consultation.
• People are autonomous.	• People are part of a hierarchy.
• People are accountable to themselves.	• People are accountable to the group.

When faced with cultural components, there are choices. One can select from one of the following options:

- **Adopt** the cultural core value and assume it as one's own while leaving one's own core value behind. This is an accommodating approach.

- **Adapt** by learning to adjust one's behavior to be in accordance with cultural norms when appropriate and changing one's own behavior to fit the environment. This is a cooperative approach.

- **Maintain** by holding on to one's own cultural norms no matter what the cultural norm is within the organization or community. This is a competitive approach.

- **Combine** cultural norms and create one's own culture based on the multiple cultures that are presented within the organization or community. This is a collaborative approach.

When determining the approach that best meets the needs of the organization, community or situation, one must be conscious of the human tendency toward "normative behavior," which is perceiving the world through one's own filter and assuming that one's own norm is *the norm*. Maintaining a sense of curiosity is critical to reaping the benefits of workplace difference as well as leveraging them for the benefit of the organization and the individuals within the organization.

Verbal and Nonverbal Communication

Verbal communication refers to one's tone, dialect, language, nuances such as slang, the pace with which one speaks, and how a person utilizes (or does not utilize) interruptions. All of these verbal communication characteristics are developed at a young age and are highly influenced by culture. In his book, *When Culture Collide: Leading Across Cultures*, author Richard D. Lewis writes:[70]

> American speech is quick, mobile and opportunistic, reflecting the speed and agility of the young country. The wisecrack is basic to their discourse. American humor excels in quips, barbed retorts and repartee, typical of the dog-eat-dog society of early America.

Lewis goes on to explain that exaggeration and hyperbole are core elements of American expressions, which contrasts with the "understated nature of the British." The United States is a melting pot of cultures and developing self-awareness about one's own verbal communication and the effect it has on others is paramount to establishing and maintaining relationships that are consistent with one's intent and that reduce conflict while fostering peace.

Of course, communication is a simultaneous exchange of verbal and nonverbal communication in a two-way process involving the listening habits of all those involved in the communication. When people are in conflict and there is a need to determine veracity, truth and meaning, the words used actually hold the least importance in determining meaning. In conflict[71] …

- Words have about 7 percent of meaning
- Tone and inflection have about 38 percent of meaning
- Facial expressions have about 55 percent of meaning

There are several aspects of nonverbal communication worth noting:

- Kinesics — an umbrella term to describe body language, gestures, eye contact, physical space, facial expression, clothes, posture and how one uses silence
- Proxemics — a term used to describe the use of physical space to convey messages
- Chronemics — a term used to describe how people use time (i.e., monochronic and polychronic)

The above demonstrates that kinesics and proxemics can influence as much as 93 percent of the communication, which is why having awareness of and sensitivity to cultural differences is paramount to communicating effectively. Creating diverse cultures requires an intentional focus on cross-cultural training to ensure that how one uses verbal and nonverbal communication enhances understanding of the message rather than detracts from it. In the western societies, the following kinesics are generally understood in the following ways:[7]

- An open limb positions indicates there is receptivity toward what is being communicated

- Crossed or folded limbs indicate defensiveness toward what is being expressed
- Forward-leaning body posture indicates attentiveness to the speaker
- A backward stance indicates an indifference to what the speaker is communicating
- An open and palm up hand gesture tends to indicate honesty
- A closed fist or pointed fingers suggests aggression or a threatening attitude
- Direct eye contact tends to indicate sincerity, openness and honesty
- An averted gaze with an avoidance of eye contact tends to indicate deceit, guilt or embarrassment

A general understanding of proxemic norms within the United States can also be helpful in ensuring one's message is communicated and experienced in a manner consistent with the intent.[73]

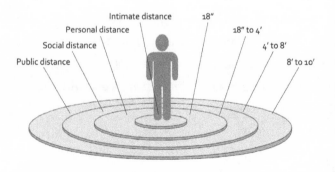

Adapted from Figure 7–3: Personal Space Categories for Those in the United States

- Intimate distance is used for very confidential communications
- Personal distance is used for talking with family and close friends
- Social distance is used to handle most business transactions
- Public distance is used when calling across the room or speaking to a group

Chromenics

A person's relationship with time can have a significant impact on cross-cultural communications — whether in relating individually with people of diverse cultural heritages or in relating to the culture of an organization and how that particular organization "does time." Understanding that not all people experience and relate to time the same way is critical to properly relating with and managing people in a work environment. There are essentially two different processing styles when it comes to time: monochronic (not to be confused with monochromatic) and polychronic.

Individuals with a monochronic processing style tend to think very linearly, sequentially and in an organized manner. Monochronic people are most at ease when they know what to expect. They thrive in meetings with agendas and with meeting leaders who adhere to an agenda. They are likely to read the table of contents of a book so that they are able to plan for what they will be learning and level set on how the information will be presented. For monochronic people, time is very quantifiable. A monochronic person will use phrases such as: "This is costing a lot of time;" "This is a waste of time;"

"Who has time for this?" etc. Time is a valuable commodity to be used judiciously. Monochronic preople often take a moralistic approach to time. Being tardy may be perceived as a flaw in one's character or experienced as rude. It could easily cost someone an opportunity such as a sale, a new job or the opportunity to acquire a new project. People who are punctual may be attributed characteristics that shed a positive light on the person such as trustworthy, reliable, etc.

In contrast, polychronic people perceive time as relational. A person with a polychronic style simultaneously processes issues in a nonlinear approach while also juggling different topics or conversations without difficulty. Time is equally important to polychronic people as it is monochronic people in that they want the time to be equitable in terms of quality, but they are not hooked on the clock. Polychronic processors are "whole picture thinkers" and are able to see how everything relates together. People with a polychronic processing style may often be late to meetings or may arrive late to the office, etc., because the activity or person with whom they are engaged with *in that moment* takes priority over an agenda or schedule. Meeting agendas may or may not be followed, and if the meeting starts late or runs late, the polychronic person is not likely to be affected by it. A polychronic person may read several books at a time; he or she may jump around in a book reading the chapters in the order of interest rather than in the order of presentation. The table on the following page demonstrates how monochronic and polychronic processing styles differ.

Most people do not strictly or exclusively process time one way or another. Most people are on a scale that leans to

MONOCHRONIC	POLYCHRONIC
• Processes one thing at a time and in sequential order	• Can process many things at once in a non-linear approach
• Wants to finish one project before beginning another	• Does not need closure when moving to the next step
• Take time commitments such as deadlines and appointments seriously	• Time commitments are an objective to be achieved
• Tends to be low context (i.e., there is a need information)	• High context, already have information
• Adhere religiously to plans	• Change plans often and easily
• Accustomed to short-termed relationships	• Builds lifetime relationships

Adapted from www.jackvan.com and the work of Edward Hall, *Hidden Dimensions of Time*

some degree in the direction of monochronic or polychronic. Understanding chromenics is critical to culturally diverse work environments because of the way in which it affects almost all aspects of working and relating.

Collaborative work environments should incorporate both chromenic styles and utilize language that is comfortable for both styles. When a person's own processing style is in conflict with the organization's cultural style, conflict can erupt. For example, I once worked with a CEO who was highly monochronic. He would request a meeting by asking for time. "May I have 30 seconds of your time?" And that is exactly how much time he would take. He highly valued multitasking in meetings because he perceived it as a judicious "use of time." And if a person was not at least 10 minutes early to a meeting, he perceived that person as late. If the person arrived exactly on time, he would be in a foul mood because he felt offended by the person's rude behavior. Actually being late would most likely result in a lost opportunity to work with him. Being a highly monochronic person, I was experienced by this CEO as someone who was of good moral character, respectful of others, smart and a real wiz at getting things done. Shortly after that project, I worked with another organization whose CEO (and subsequently the entire organizational culture) was highly polychronic. Meetings rarely started on time and seldom ended on time. Time was fluid and whatever one was doing in the moment was of the utmost importance. As a result, people spent a great deal of time waiting for each other, and rarely expressed agitation about doing so. What was especially notable was how multitasking was perceived within the culture. It was perhaps the single rudest thing a person could do. Multitasking was experienced as "not paying attention," "disrespecting the person who was speaking," and easily became the topic du jour around the water cooler. Multitasking could easily result in outsider status.

Neither processing style is better than the other. However, the propensity for time management to become a catalyst for conflict is so great, it is imperative that those individuals tasked with cultivating a positive, productive and diverse culture understand the importance of incorporating both styles within the organization in order to nurture a peace-promoting workplace.

Gender

Men and women communicate differently — at home and at work. These gender-based communication differences can be the catalyst to not only miscommunication but also conflict, including bullying behavior, lack of upward mobility within the organization as well as disparity in workload allocation.

Misunderstandings often occur due to the *delivery* of the message rather than the *content* of the message. Therefore, understanding how differences in communication by feminine and masculine genders affect outcomes is essential to creating peace in the workplace.

Use of language is one of the most consistent ways in which people of masculine and feminine genders communicate differently. Dr. Deborah Tannen, author of *Talking From 9 to 5: Women and Men at Work*, explains that women or people with a female gender often use conversation as a vehicle for establishing relationships. Conversation, therefore, is a tool for building rapport with one another. "Rapport talk" is intended to build relationships, strengthen connections and foster a positive relationship with one another. It is not intended as a vehicle for reporting data or important work-related information. In contrast, men and individuals with a masculine gender rely much less on "rapport talk" and instead focus on "report talk" — a form of communication that's sole purpose is to share information. Therefore, when women in engage in rapport talk and men hear it as report talk, they respond with attempts to remedy the problem. This often causes great frustration for women who were not seeking a solution but rather an opportunity for connection.

Hedging is another way in which women tend to downplay or soften opposing positions or ideas. Rather than directly stating, "That's not a good idea. I would like for us to try it this way," a woman might reply stating, "Perhaps we should try it another way?" While this *sounds* like a question, it may actually be a directive. Women tend to hedge when communicating with a person in a lower power position in order to achieve a particular goal while also maintaining the relationship. While men do use hedging as a communication tactic, they tend to do so with people of higher power. In the workplace where men and women are constantly communicating, it is important to be able to discern the difference between hedging — i.e., trying to achieve a goal with sensitivity to a relationship — and actual uncertainty. Hedging can become problematic when it is perceived as uncertainty or lack of understanding of the problem and the potential solutions.

In her book, Tannen explains the concept of ritual fight, referred to as "ritual opposition." Tannen explains that men are more likely than women to engage in "agonism" — "a warlike, oppositional format" intended to accomplish a "range of interactional goals that have nothing literally to do with fighting."[74] This process involves mustering all the arguments possible to defend a particular position while simultaneously undercutting and attacking the opposing person or viewpoint. In an article titled, "Negotiating Like a Woman: How Gender Impacts Communication Between the Sexes" authors Nina Meierding and Jan Frankel Shau explain, "While women tend to hedge more than men, men tend to use ritual opposition more than women (except in the world of trial lawyers, where both sexes may excel in this style of argumentation)."[75] The authors explain that ritual opposition is not designed to lob personal attacks or denigrate the opposing person or viewpoint; it is simply aimed at winning an argument. The exclusive focus on winning does so at the cost of rapport building, creating and fostering positive relationships and allowing the opposing party the opportunity to save face. The aggressive nature of ritual opposition lends itself to being experienced as a personal attack or insult.

Gender differences affect more than how men and women speak; they impact the way in which they listen too. When women listen, they have a tendency to nod their heads in what looks like agreement. While nodding they may also add small insertions such as "right," "I understand," "OK," etc. The nodding and inclusion of verbal insertions while listening is not intended to be communicated as agreement, but rather an indication that the she is listening. It is an attempt to validate, encourage and inspire continued communication so that the she is able to acquire the information being expressed. This overlapping style of speech is often understood by men as an interruption, and perhaps even as an indication that the woman agrees with him. It is obvious to see how this can create conflict.

In her book, Tannen writes, "Conversation is a ritual. We say things that seem the thing to say, without thinking of the literal meaning of our words any more than we expect the question, 'How are you?' to call forth a detailed account of aches and pains." In this manner, women are habitual apologizers in a way that men simply are not. Women say, "I am sorry" for almost everything. If a woman is walking in the door at the same time as another person, chances are she will say, "I am sorry" even though she did nothing wrong and there was no mishap that should beckon an apology from anyone. Women tend to express concern and empathy through apologies. In contrast, men tend to only apologize when they have failed at a responsibility or they are at fault in an actual error. This incongruity in how apologies are utilized is confusing for both men and women. Men can become conditioned to believing the woman is actually at fault while women become calloused to the fact that men rarely, if ever, "take responsibility." Meierding and Shau explain the disconnect this way: "Men may assume a woman is accepting fault and taking responsibility when she apologizes, but she may simply be trying to restore a relationship or build rapport." Ultimately, when a woman apologizes unnecessarily she positions herself in a role of less authority — one that is ultimately diminutive in nature. Apologies can cause a person to experience vulnerability. When women apply rapport apologies in order to mend relationships or extend empathy and understanding, they are waiting for reciprocity. When the reciprocity does not happen, there is a shift in power that can cause damage in the short and long term. From the concept of peace building, this self-diminishing habit jeopardizes a woman's dignity.

Apologies are important and should be taken seriously when they are, in fact, necessary. Understanding the difference among the types of apologies is important so that they can be applied appropriately and with integrity.

- A **rapport apology** is a non-accountability apology intended as a relationship builder; however, this type of apology can create miscommunications.
- A **full apology** is a recognition of a harm done; it demonstrates regret while acknowledging how the actions may have felt to the harmed party; it is a

promise not to repeat it and a request to repair the harm.

- A **cohesion apology** is an expression of regret with the goal of mending a relationship or situation but falls short of a full apology in that it is not an admonishment of guilt, and therefore, attempts to repair the harm may be minimal or non-existent.

- A **dispersion apology** is a tactic used to get out of a negative situation and to be rid of the guilt of the situation. It an attempt to disperse one's self of a situation and is not an act of integrity and will not foster collaboration.

- A **partial apology** is an expression of remorse or regret without an attempt to repair the harm.

Apologies can be perceived as a loss of face, and therefore they are often met with resistance in the workplace. However, where there has been harm done, good faith attempts at repairing are is necessary for promoting peace in the workplace.

BRIDGING DIFFERENCES

Differences in the workplace are positive and should be embraced — for both humanitarian reasons and because they positively impact an organization's culture and indirectly its bottom line. Barriers to embracing differences should be quickly recognized and addressed. The following are just a few barriers to look for:

- Assuming superiority
- Assuming differences
- Stereotyping, prejudice and racism
- Different communication patterns
- Stories of victimization and demonization
- Lack of ownership (i.e., that is "someone else's problem")

Strategies for embracing differences include:

- Developing cultural awareness
- Being mindful of stereotypes
- Listening to understand
- Being attuned and open to cultural differences
- Focusing on one's own culture to understand another's
- Enjoying differences
- Separating culture from exploitation

The Equal Employment Opportunity Commission created by the Civil Rights Act of 1964 "prohibits discrimination based on race, color, national origin, sex and religion, and also prohibits employers from retaliating against any employee who exercises his or her rights under Title VII."[76] But "protecting from discrimination" is obviously not synonymous with embracing diversity. Organizations that embrace differences in the workplace reap the rewards through increased innovation, increased creativity, enhanced recruiting efforts and a decreased in employee turnover.[77] All of these benefit the organization as well as the individuals within the organization, and ultimately, the communities in which they live. Differences in the workplace are not just good for business; they are good for people.

CHAPTER FIVE

BE THE CHANGE
CREATING CULTURES OF PEACE

To cultivate peace, senior leadership must adopt the identity of a peacemaker and assume the responsibilities that come with the role.

FROM FORTUNE 500S TO SINGLE OWNER-OPERATED businesses, creating a culture of peace is a top down process led by the most senior leadership — most notably the CEO whose vision (or lack thereof) for the organization creates a ripple effect throughout every aspect of the company. While focusing on culture may feel like the soft side of business, it is one of the most important aspects of creating a thriving, profitable organization that attracts and retains the best talent and delivers a superior customer experience. Some of the most successful companies — Google, Apple and Southwest Airlines — are highly focused and committed to company culture. Leadership at these organizations know that the values, norms and beliefs embodied by the organization are paramount to success, which is why they commit thoughtful analysis and consistent attention to developing, implementing and maintaining organizational culture.

The development of an organization's culture should address questions such as: What central values are important to the company? What communication strategies need to be implemented to communicate these values to the teams within the organization? How might the values be communicated in a way that resonates with individuals within the organization so they become a source of inspiration and motivation and provide the opportunity for individuals to contribute to something greater than self? How can cultural values become actionable and have a direct impact on day-to-day operations? The development of a culture of peace must address all the questions above as well as questions such as: How do the organization's values ensure the dignity of the individuals within the organization as well as the dignity of those individuals the organization affects in the marketplace? What policies need to be implemented in order to ensure a culture of peace that translates into a peaceful presence in the marketplace?

The responses to these questions will shape the development of a company's vision and mission and influence how the culture will evolve over time. The reality is that every organization has a culture. That culture is either developed strategically or it evolves organically. Those organizations that fall in the latter category tend to have employees (and customers) who fail to find purpose, meaning or inspiration in the organization. They may also evolve into a "Lord of the Flies" environment in which those individuals who garner power through aggression and bullying tactics hold power over those whose work styles are more collaborative, causing high levels of conflict within the organization. This can have a devastating impact on employee engagement and retention, morale, creativity, productivity and, ultimately, profits.

CULTIVATING PEACE FROM THE TOP DOWN

While it is always helpful to engage consultants with unique expertise in helping organizations develop and deploy vision, mission and values with an intent to cultivate peace, the following are general considerations for creating a culture that honors the need for human security (in and outside the organization) while also encouraging individuals to work and interact in a manner that is authentic to the organization's vision, mission and values.

First and foremost, senior management must display the characteristics of exemplary leadership without which all attempts at cultivating peace will be experienced by the individuals within the organization as inauthentic — all words and no action. Senior leadership must adopt the identity of a peacemaker and assume the responsibilities that come with the role seriously. The five tenets of leadership are tenets all peacemakers should know and adhere to.

1. **Model the way**. The leadership team is responsible for developing the values, norms and beliefs that shape the company culture, including how individuals inside and outside the organization should be treated and the way goals should be pursued. Once these standards are established, members of the leadership team must set the example for others to follow —authentically and consistently. This means that there is no longer an "it's just business" approach to managing people.

Peace building requires that one behave as a human rather than a particular role (i.e., CEO, vice president, manager, etc.) To accomplish and minimize fear that often arises during periods of change, modeling the way also requires that interim goals are established to allow others to achieve small wins as they work toward larger objectives, creating opportunities for success.

2. **Inspire a shared vision**. Cultivating a culture of peace requires that every member of the leadership team passionately believes in his or her ability to be an agent of positive change. They envision the future and actively pursue strategies and tactics to create an ideal and unique image of what the organization can evolve into. Their passion serves to enlist others to share in this vision.

3. **Challenge the process**. Cultivating a culture of peace requires that the leadership team search for opportunities to challenge the status quo with absolute integrity and respect for all those who might be affected. They seek to elevate the experience of everyone within the organization as well as how the organization is experienced in the marketplace. Inherently this requires experimentation and the courage to take risks. When these risks do not result as hoped or intended, leaders committed to cultivating peace choose to perceive the experience as an opportunity for learning rather than an opportunity to shame and blame others.

4. **Enable others to act.** Peace-building leaders seek every opportunity to foster collaboration in the workplace, accepting the fact that doing so requires investments in time and resources. They understand that respect and teamwork sustain extraordinary efforts. Leaders committed to peace building strive to create a workplace in which people feel trusted and valued. They want people to experience dignity both in how they contribute to the organization as well as in their work relationships. They seek opportunities to strengthen others so that each individual is able to feel both capable and powerful.

5. **Encourage the heart.** Creating a culture of peace that results in extraordinary outcomes is hard work, which is why exemplary leaders recognize the contributions that individuals within the organization make. To create a strong, productive and inspired team, the members need to share in the rewards of their efforts. Celebrating efforts is one of the most powerful ways to lift up others and foster a spirit of unity.

Second, senior leadership must exercise transparency and set clear expectations. The first step in doing this is to establish a vision for what a culture of peace looks like and identify what the vision is intended to accomplish as well as what sort of behaviors and attitudes are valued by the organization and those that are not acceptable. This vision for the company culture should be documented so as to preserve the integrity of the message as well as to identify how it will be brought to life operationally. Establishing clear expectations and holding formal discussions about the vision can help to minimize confusion or potential deviations from it. Establishing clear expectations will help the meaning and purpose of the vision to become tangible and real for individuals within the organization. This can also help in developing what an ideal environment looks like so as to establish steps in achieving it.

Third, creating a culture of peace requires constant attention and investment in it. Organizations should always be in a state of evolving. As an organization grows — in revenue, clients, employees, etc. — new opportunities for evolving business objectives and strategic initiatives will emerge. Growth requires investments in recruiting, onboarding, real estate, office space, IT, etc.; it also requires ongoing organizational training to ensure the vision, mission and values evolve with the company and the spirit and integrity of them are preserved and experienced throughout every aspect of the organization.

Fourth, creating a culture of peace in the workplace requires hiring individuals who are compatible with the vision, mission and values of an organization. Hiring someone who is highly skilled in a particular area and known for "getting results" but who also has a reputation for achieving those results at any cost may create disruptions in the corporate culture that cause directly related and indirectly related conflict. Hiring practices should include question sets that score how well a person fits with the culture; how likely they are to embrace and champion the culture; and whether or not they will strengthen it or create challenges to continuity. During the interview process inquire about the following:

- Ask questions that help uncover what motivates and inspires the person
- Ask questions that help uncover how the person manages conflict
- Explore how the person behaves in high-stress environments
- Ask for examples of when something did not go as planned to find out how the person handled it
- Ask questions that help uncover how the person manages a conflict with high stakes

The answers to these questions can provide insight into whether or not this person will fit well in a culture designed to cultivate human security and human dignity. Asking this question pointedly is also helpful: What type of culture are you looking for and think will enhance your contributions?

VISION, MISSION AND VALUES

Creating a Mission Statement That Inspires Peace

A good mission statement clearly identifies why an organization exists. This statement is a much higher level statement than "we exist to transform xyz widget" or "we exist to deliver xyz services," and instead identifies why what an organization does matters in the marketplace, in the lives of the organization's stakeholders and ultimately, in the world. For example, under the leadership of Steve Jobs, Apple's mission was "To make a contribution to the world by making tools for the mind that advance humankind."[78] Now *that* is a great reason to exist. This statement provides a mission that contributes to humanity and allows freedom for the "how" to evolve as the industry (and human) needs change and as opportunities and needs for innovation emerge. It inspires employees and stakeholders to participate in contributing to and experiencing something greater than self. And, ultimately, if one intends to participate in the advancement of humankind, the language of the mission statement must be supportive of the notions associated with peace — dignity and security, which "making tools for the mind that advances humankind" accomplishes. Under Apple's new leadership, the mission statement has changed to "Apple designs Macs, the best personal computer in the world, along with OS X, iLife, iWork and professional software. Apple leads the digital music revolution with its iPods and iTunes online store. Apple reinvented the mobile phone with its revolutionary iPhone and App store, and is defining the future of mobile media and computing devices with iPad."[79] This new mission statement is a laundry list of what Apple does. It is boastful, self-serving and completely void of any language that might inspire stakeholders to come together to participate in something greater than self. Mission statements that list what a company does paired with statements about how well they do it will not easily lend themselves to peace-promoting cultures because the focus is on the company and not on those to whom the company seeks to bring value or the contribution the company seeks to make in the world. These types of mission statements encourage a bottom line, get-results-at-any-cost approach to business.

While Apple's vision under Steve Jobs indeed contributed to the advancement of humanity — through their products and nnovative ways of bringing products to market — resulting in a cult-like following from consumers and American employees alike, the company committed human rights violations in Chinese manufacturing facilities and continues to do so as of the time of this book's publication. Violations such as "unpaid labor, unreasonable fines, 12-hour shifts six days a week and unhygienic living conditions" are among the violations listed in a 2015 China Labor Watch (CLW) that was a follow up to a 2013 report that notes these same violation.[80] The contribution Apple has brought to the marketplace has truly elevated the human experience, yet they have done so at the expense of employees. Creating a culture of peace requires that all stakeholders experience human security and have the ability to live a life of dignity that is free of fear. Apple still has much work to do in this area.

Creating a Vision Statement That Inspires Peace

A vision statement articulates what a company wants to be known for. This is an opportunity to stake a claim on the legacy an organization wants to create for itself as a result of its mission. The vision is not goal setting or creating a futuristic image of what the vision will be five, 10 or 20 years down the road. It is also not a laundry list of how the organization hopes to accomplish its mission. Rather, it is a statement that identifies the lasting impact the organization intends to make in the industry, the community and the world or perhaps to humanity. Great vision statements create an emotional connection that resonates with the individuals within the organization as well as with its stakeholders. In his book, *The Innovation Secrets of Steve Jobs*, author Carmine Gallo describes a vision statement as, "a picture of a better world that your product or service makes possible. Captivating visions inspire investors, employees and customers — and best of all, they inspire those stakeholders to become evangelists for the organization." Gallo asserts that a vision should meet three criteria: it should be specific, concise and consistent.[81]

In his book, Gallo tells the story of when Google went looking for venture capital. At the time, they expressed their vision as, "to provide access to the world's information in one click." Gallo claims, "that one sentence was so inspiring that investors at the Silicon Valley venture firm not only funded the company but also now require any entrepreneur who sets foot into the office to articulate the company's vision in 10 words or fewer." One venture capitalist explained to Gallo, "If you can't describe what you do in 10 words or fewer, I'm not buying, I'm not investing, I'm not interested. Period." Apple's original vision under the leadership of Steve Jobs was "a computer in the hands of everyday people." He set this vision at a time when most computers were as expensive as they were complex. The average American was no more likely to understand them as they were to afford them. These vision statements have truly become the legacy of these two organizations, and many might agree that their contributions to the advancement of humanity and human security are significant. Google and Apple both created a vision that inspired others to enlist in these visions of what might be, so much so that together they brought the vision to fruition. Contrast the early version of Apple's vision with today's vision for Apple set forth by CEO Tim Cook:

We believe that we are on the face of the earth to make great products and that's not changing. We are constantly focusing on innovating. We believe in the simple not the complex. We believe that we need to own and control the primary technologies behind the products that we make, and participate only in markets where we can make a significant contribution. We believe in saying no to thousands of projects, so that we can really focus on the few that are truly important and meaningful to us. We believe in deep collaboration and cross-pollination of our groups, which allow us to innovate in a way that others cannot. And frankly, we don't settle for anything less than excellence in every group in the company, and we have the self- honesty to admit when we're wrong and the courage to change. And I think regardless of who is in what job those values are so embedded in this company that Apple will do extremely well.[82]

Much like the mission statement, this vision is boastful, self-interested and void of any commitment or desire to contribute to something greater than self. It is a self-serving mission, using the word "we" 14 times. It is a vision statement that celebrates a belief in its own superiority. It is arrogant and uninspiring. This vision will not inspire a culture of peace; it does not inspire a vision of elevating human dignity; and it establishes a zero sum expectation of winners and losers. According to

Time magazine, within a year of Job's passing the company "shed more than $100 billion in market capitalization." A year later the stock was down by 10 percent even as "the tech-heavy NASDAQ index has soared by more than 20 percent."[83]

People rally behind visions that inspire the ability to contribute to something greater than self. Inherent to human nature is a deep desire to live a life of purpose. Most Americans dedicate more of their time to professional work than they do any other activity — even sleep. Therefore, the ability to contribute in any meaningful way to society, humanity and the world is best achieved through one's professional endeavors. Companies that understand this concept and develop a mission and vision statement that support the human desire to contribute to something greater than self will inspire people to be more than individuals exchanging their time and knowledge for money; they will inspire people to be partners committed to a shared vision of positive change.

Creating Core Values That Inspire Peace

Core values are deeply ingrained principles that inform how individuals within an organization work and conduct themselves. They inform the strategies the organization will employ to fulfill its mission. They are the cornerstone of a company's culture and are designed to bring the mission and vision to fruition. Core values are intended to be guardrails that keep the company on track and focused on its mission and vision, and therefore, they can never be compromised for economic or short-term gain. The core values are what help to shape a company's distinctiveness in the market, in the minds of employees, and in the experience the customer has with the company.

In a *Harvard Business Review* article titled, "Make Your Values Mean Something," Patrick Lencioni, leadership consultant and *New York Times* best-selling author, explains that there are three types of core values CEOs and senior leadership teams should be aware of when engaging a core values initiative:[84]

1. **Aspirational values** are the values a company currently lacks but wants to establish in order to succeed in the future. For example, changing market demands and industry trends may present a need for creating a new value. When an organization makes the strategic decision to cultivate a culture of peace, creating aspirational values may be necessary to bridge the current culture to the culture the organization aspires to become.

2. **Permission-to-play values** reflect the behavioral and social expectations of all individuals within the organization. Permission-to-play values tend to be a standard set up values that do not allow for much differentiation in the marketplace. However, these can be significant opportunities for differentiation when the permission-to-play values are intentionally designed to cultivate peace in the workplace.

3. **Accidental values** are those values that arise organically without the intentional cultivation of the leadership. Accidental values typically represent the

common interests that exist among individuals with an organization. For example, the HR director of a small, owner-operated business was a huge sports fanatic. As a result, all of the team building activities, internal communications, employee recognition programs, etc. were themed around sports. The unintended consequence of these activities was that it created an accidental value of competition — pitting people against one another in fierce zero sum competitions and alienating those who had no interest in sports. Within that organization, a subculture of inclusivity emerged to address the alienation and competitiveness that had become so pervasive. These opposing values were confusing to the individuals within the organization and had a negative impact on morale as well as a negative impact on employee engagement.

The development and rollout of core values are too often presented as a onetime event, and the success of the core values is determined by the initial attention the core values receive. The authenticity of the content of the values is what will determine their success, and authenticity is something that can only be experienced. When core values are rolled out, individuals within the organization will immediately look to leadership to determine if the organization is serious or not. Leadership is solely responsible for the success or failure of core values. If leadership does not "walk the talk" immediately, consistently and with 100 percent compliance, the credibility of the leadership team will be undermined and the core values themselves will become irrelevant at best and a joke at worst.

To be a vehicle for cultivating peace and a tool for true differentiation, core values need to go far beyond bland, common sense, generic ideals such as "passion, integrity and teamwork." In fact, according Lencioni's *Harvard Business Review* article, "55 percent of all Fortune 100 companies claim integrity is a core value, 49 percent espouse customer satisfaction, and 40 percent tout teamwork."[85] Integrity, customer service and teamwork are a given in today's business environment. Without those three values underpinning the day-to-day operations, work would not get done and businesses would not make ends meet. These generic values not only fail to contribute meaningfully to the organization or the marketplace, they can be the underlying source of poor employee engagement and, ultimately, a mediocre customer experience.

Core values are intended to bring the mission and vision to life; therefore, the development of core values is inherently a visionary exercise. Too often the development of core values is turned into a feel-good, consensus building exercise, which is not only not the point of core values, but it is also does not net the best results. Values initiatives should be about developing a fundamental, strategically sound set of beliefs from which to build an intentional culture. Just as a CEO is unlikely to engage a consensus-driven decision-making process for go-to-market strategies, finance strategies or operational planning, developing the company culture in this manner will not net the best result, either. Surveying all individuals within the organization conveys the message that all input is equally valuable, that the individuals who comprise the company are the same people who should lead the vision for the company, and it implies (usually incorrectly) that the input provided will be implemented. All input is not equally valuable because the majority of the organization does not have the insight into the strategic planning that is necessary to chart the path for creating it. They also do not have the training or expertise to take on the task of planning how to best bring the vision to life. When people are asked for their input, there is a very basic and fair expectation that their input will be used in some form or fashion. When it is not incorporated into the final set of values, resentment can occur because the individual does not feel honored or respected.

The senior leadership team, who has access to the visions and strategic planning set forth by the CEO, along with the CEO, members of the c-suite and any founders who may still be a part of the company are the group of individuals who should drive a core values initiative. This team should engage a consultant to facilitate the dialogues and ensure the team has carefully thought through the implications of each core value in consideration. The consultant can also help the team to massage the values so they support both the strategic initiatives of the organization while also fostering a culture of human dignity and security for all stakeholders. This process takes time. It is not likely to emerge from an afternoon off-site meeting or a weekend retreat. The core values are intended to shape the culture of the organization and play a critical role in the legacy of the company as well as its contributions to the marketplace and perhaps even humanity. This should be given ample time for discussion, reflection and contemplation.

Once the core values are developed and agreed upon, they need to be integrated into every employee-related process: recruiting, hiring, onboarding, performance management systems, criteria for promotions and recognition, as well as termination policies. At every touch point within an organization, the core values must be experienced in real and tangible ways so individuals within the organization become conditioned to operating from these values consistently and understand the core values serve as the basis for every organizational decision.

CREATING A LEARNING CULTURE

Bringing the mission, vision and values to life via swag such as coffee mugs, T-shirts and mouse pads can be a fun way to get them in front of people, but these are superfluous and not likely to have impact. When a company *is modeling* the core values at every level of business, swag is likely to be neutral in terms of effectiveness. However, when the company *is not modeling* the core values at every level of business, swag can actually cause harm because it becomes a constant reminder of just how big of a joke the core values are.

Creating a culture of learning is an important aspect of vision building and bringing the core values to life. The best laid plans remain only that when there is no implementation strategy to bring it to life. The following are ways to create a culture of learning designed to bring the core values to life and make them meaningful and relevant to the individuals within an organization.

- **Develop and implement a core values curriculum** that demonstrates how the core values come to life in day-to-day, real-life scenarios. A professional trainer who has expertise in neuroscience and the ability to develop training materials in a brain sensitive manner should develop the training curriculum. That means incorporating techniques that foster collaboration and peaceful ways of problem-solving as well as resolving workplace disputes. This person should then be engaged to train key stakeholders within the organization who can model the values in real-life scenarios, be evangelists for the values and train others via mentorship programs.

- **Create a mentorship program** that serves two purposes: 1) to help existing employees understand how to integrate the core values in their day-to-day work; 2) to educate new hires on the core values and expectations for bringing them to life. The mentorship program should include a train-the-trainer program that positions trainers in every functional area of the organization.

- Learning cultures **give people permission to make mistakes**. In a fear-driven culture where mistakes are opportunities for shaming and placing blame, people become risk adverse. In order to learn and grow, mistakes must be embraced and put in the context of learning. When an organization gives space for mistakes, people are then free to share their own mistakes and the knowledge that was acquired as a result. One person's mistake becomes a learning opportunity for others, which ultimately minimizes error and optimizes innovation.

- Get out of silos and **review projects as a team**. Allowing the time and space for reviewing project from beginning to end allows all team members the ability to examine the processes and decision making and reflect on areas for improvement while acknowledging what worked and why. Gain clarity on if what was expected occurred and compare that with what actually occurred. The learning is in the space between expectations and reality.

- **Invite opposing perspectives** and listen to them with the intent to understand rather than the intent to defend. Explore perspective on how a project or decision may impact the business (i.e., market share, profit, etc.), the customer experience and the brand. Explore how each of these perspectives incorporate the organization's core values and seek to find the solutions that move the needle in terms of the mission and vision.

Creating a culture of learning is an important way to not just gain a better grasp on individual topics, but it also allows the interconnection of issues to emerge. As individuals within the organization begin to understand the interconnected structure of their work and how day-to-day business operations can connect back to the vision, mission and values, they begin to experience their own contributions in more meaningful ways. This also allows serves as a means of deepening trust and collaboration, which ultimately increases performance.

Culture-driven organizations inspire a sense of purpose and unity among stakeholders — employees, customers, vendor partners and even shareholders. Knowing that one is playing a role in bringing something of value to the marketplace is a rewarding experience. When an organization's culture elevates the human experience and honors the need for security and dignity for all those it touches, it moves beyond being a positive contributor to the marketplace and becomes an agent of positive change in the world.

CHAPTER SIX

PEACE IN PRACTICE
IMPLEMENTING ALTERNATIVE DISPUTE RESOLUTION PRACTICES

Substituting the traditional processes for managing grievances and policy violations with peace-promoting practices to conflict resolution demonstrates to employees that their needs, their development and their concerns are respected by the workplace community and that opportunities for human growth and development exist.

"PEACE DOES NOT MEAN AN absence of conflicts; differences will always be there. Peace means solving these differences through peaceful means; through dialogue, education, knowledge; and through humane ways." This quote by the Dalai Lama demonstrates the need for rethinking how organizations typically intervene in conflict. Punitive systems designed to diminish, separate, instill fear, shame or, worse, constructively terminate, individuals who need guidance in realizing their potential or clarity in the expectations of them perpetuate unproductive conflict.

This chapter presents alternative dispute resolution interventions that can transform how conflict is experienced in the workplace so that it can be experienced as opportunities for connection and growth — at the personal, professional and organizational levels. The following are specific ways organizations can create peace in the workplace and transform conflict into collaboration.

- **Conflict management training** provides opportunities for individuals to grow in their leadership skills by learning peace-promoting techniques for navigating conflict effectively and productively so that they may be agents of positive change in their personal and professional lives.

- **Mediation** is a process in which an impartial third party helps individuals experiencing a dispute to discover a mutually agreed upon solution to their conflict. With mediation, parties have equal input into the mediation process and the settlement terms, which may be litigated or non-litigated conflict. The mediator facilitates the resolution process and has no authority to impose a settlement without both parties' agreement. During mediation all parties are able to exchange information, express desired expectations and propose solutions for reaching resolution. The mediator facilitates this process by helping the parties communicate effectively. All parties must agree to participate in the mediation process in good faith. Having a mediator on retainer — and even on speed dial — can help organizations manage conflicts as soon as they emerge, mitigating risks for the individuals, the work environment and the organization.

- **Facilitation** is an effective way to resolve group conflicts through the use of an impartial third-party facilitator. The facilitator's role is to support this process by providing a framework for participants to communicate clearly and appropriately. The facilitator creates a structured process that allows participants equal opportunities to share their concerns and collaborate on constructive approaches to resolution. Like mediation, the facilitator has no authority to impose a settlement without agreement of the group. During facilitation all participants are provided the opportunity to exchange information, express desired expectations and propose solutions for reaching resolution or solutions to challenges the organization faces.

- **Restorative justice** is a framework for alternative dispute resolution models that focus on the needs of the individuals who have been harmed by someone else's actions, as well as the needs of the community of people who were directly or indirectly harmed. Restorative justice differs from more punitive approaches where the main objective is to punish the offending party, seeking instead to involve the offending party in repairing the harm his or her actions caused and restoring as much normalcy as possible to the harmed party. To accomplish this, the person who experienced harm takes an active role in the process, while the person who caused the harm is encouraged to take responsibility for his or her actions to repair the harm and establish an agreement on creating a new vision for the future of the relationship(s).

- **Conflict coaching** is conducted on an individual basis in a one-on-one process. Clients are able to enhance their understanding of a conflict or dispute by working with the conflict coach to learn strategies and skills for engaging with the party with whom there is a conflict.

Coaching is an effective alternative to mediation when one party refuses to attend mediation while the other party remains committed to achieving a peaceful solution.

GET AHEAD OF CONFLICT WITH CONFLICT MANAGEMENT TRAINING

Individuals who manage people or processes are confronted with near-constant conflict, which in and of itself is not bad. There are many positive attributes of conflict. The following are just a few:

- Increased understanding of others
- Increased trust
- Improved working relationships
- Better solutions to problems or challenges
- Improved team performance
- Increased motivation

However, when managers do not have the skills to productively manage conflict, the work environment can quickly become destructive and unproductive, both of which cost the organization time and money.

According to a study commissioned by CPP Inc. — publishers of the Myers-Briggs Assessment and the Thomas-Kilmann Conflict Mode Instrument — U.S. employees spend 2.1 hours per week involved with conflict, which amounts to approximately $359 billion in paid hours (based on an average hourly earnings of $17.95), or the equivalent of 385 million working days. For the purposes of the study, the authors defined conflict as: "any workplace disagreement that disrupts the flow of work." The study, titled "Workplace Conflict and How Businesses Can Harness It to Thrive," lists the following statistics to demonstrate how pervasive conflict is in the workplace:[86]

- 85 percent of employees deal with conflict on some level
- 29 percent of employees deal with it almost constantly
- 34 percent of conflict occurs among front-line employees
- 12 percent of employees say they frequently witness conflict among the senior team
- 27 percent of employees have witnessed conflicts lead to personal attacks
- 25 percent of employees have seen conflict result in sickness or absence
- 9 percent have seen workplace conflict cause a project to fail

The inability for managers to effectively navigate and resolve conflict that results in a positive resolution costs companies nearly one full day of productivity per month, per person — two and a half weeks per year, per person. It is not surprising that almost all employees recognize the critical need for conflict management skills in the workplace. In fact, the study found that 70 percent of employees believe managing conflict is a critically important leadership skill. And 54 percent of employees believe managers could handle disputes more effectively by addressing underlying tensions immediately when they surface.[87]

When managed effectively, conflict can stimulate progress, deepen trust within teams and between individuals and strengthen relationships — all of which enhances productivity and optimizes bottom line results.

Around the world, conflict resolution skills are rarely taught as core curriculum in education, which means most adults enter the workplace with little to no knowledge of how to prevent and/or manage conflict.

Training is the single most important driver for high quality outcomes to conflict. And yet the CPP Inc. study found that almost 60 percent of employees in the U.S. have never received basic conflict management and dispute resolution training. However, of those who have, 95 percent report that it has helped them to positively navigate conflict. Equally important is that almost 60 percent of workers who receive conflict management training report to seek out win-win outcomes when conflicts arise, and 85 percent of people claim to be more proactive when conflict surfaces without taking the conflict personally.[88]

Perhaps the most important fact to surface from this research is that 76 percent of employees who receive conflict management and dispute resolution training experience positive outcomes from conflict:[89]

- 41 percent developed a better understanding of others
- 29 percent found a better solution to the workplace

problem (this figure rises to 81 percent for U.S. workers)

When employees understand how to manage conflict and harness the positive powers of it, conflict can transition from a cost to the bottom line to an investment in the organization and the people who work for it. This quote from the report summarizes the positive power conflict can bring to an organization: "If organizations invest in building the awareness of self and others on which better relationships depend, they will see the energy created by interpersonal friction generate sparks of creativity, rather than consuming flames. HR, leaders, and employees must all accept their responsibility for becoming competent conflict managers."

Creating peace in the workplace requires that people have the skills to be peacemakers, which is why investing in conflict management and dispute resolution training is critical to harnessing the creative power conflict can bring to the organization. (See the Appendix for information on workplace conflict and peace building training.)

DE-ESCALATE WORKPLACE CONFLICT WITH MEDIATION

When most people think about mediation, they often think "lawsuits and litigation." And while mediation is an excellent alternative to resolving disputes that have escalated to this level, it is also an effective approach for de-escalating conflict and preventing a workplace dispute from reaching the legal system.

In order to maintain a productive and engaging workplace, managers should seek to resolve disputes immediately when they surface. Maintaining productive peer relationships is paramount to maintaining a productive and peace-promoting work environment. Mediation offers a formal process in which individuals involved in a workplace conflict can express their opinions and perspectives via a solutions-oriented, collaborative process in which all parties have influence on the outcome. Resolving workplace conflict with mediation has numerous benefits:

- **Cost benefit.** Mediation is generally less expensive when contrasted to the expense of litigation or other forms of dispute resolution, especially when mediation is implemented immediately when conflict surfaces.
- **Mutually satisfactory outcomes.** Because mediation provides all parties involved in a dispute with the ability to participate in the resolution of it, parties tend to be more satisfied and compliant with the outcome.
- **Personal empowerment.** When individuals are given the opportunity to negotiate resolutions to their own problems in the workplace, they are empowered to take what was learned in the mediation process and apply that knowledge in future conflicts. They learn the value of de-escalating conflict, which benefits the individual and the organization.
- **Preservation of relationships.** Workplace conflict can be very disruptive to the individuals involved as well as the individuals who are indirectly affected. Coworkers are often in a position to work with someone for years, perhaps even decades. Because the process of mediation addresses all parties' interests,

it can be a powerful resource for preserving working relationships in ways that would not be possible in zero-sum, win/lose decision-making procedures.

- **Lasting resolutions.** Resolving workplace conflict via mediation tends to bring about resolutions that can stand the test of time, and if a dispute occurs in the future, the parties are more likely to utilize a cooperative forum of problem-solving to resolve their differences rather than pursue an adversarial approach.

Managers should initiate mediation as soon as a complaint or conflict surfaces to their attention. Implementing mediation at the earliest stage demonstrates to employees that their complaints are taken seriously, that how they experience their role in the organization matters, and that the organization's commitment to creating a culture of peace is real and reliable. Early implementation minimizes the negative ripple effect that can quickly manifest within the organization while also minimizing the negative impact on those involved in the conflict. Most importantly, early implementation of mediation has the potential to not just resolve conflict, but also heal the divide that allowed the conflict to surface.

FOSTER A COLLABORATIVE WORK ENVIRONMENT WITH FACILITATION

Facilitation is a way for organizations to work more effectively, productively and collaboratively together while seeking to accomplish specific goals within the context of a meeting or series of meetings. Facilitators help groups get past positional thinking and personal agendas in order to surface the underlying issues critical to the problem, conflict or business matter they seek to resolve.

Facilitation is designed to build consensus and foster group cohesion in the group's journey to arriving at their common goal. This may be within the context of a conflict, or it may be initiated as a means of achieving consensus in strategic planning, the creation of vision, mission, values or other business-related issues that cannot or should not be tackled in a silo.

Facilitation is an excellent intervention to prevent conflict or to mitigate the risks of it in its earliest stages. Unlike mediation, which follows a set process that is determined by the mediator, in facilitation the group determines both the process as well as the outcome. The facilitator assists by providing structured brainstorming as well as techniques for optimal group thinking and group collaboration, keeping the group on track and focused on creation of options and ideas while recording and documenting the process.

The facilitator is responsible for designing, organizing and progressing meetings while helping to alleviate tensions and supporting participants in achieving a collaborative, solutions-focused mindset. Facilitated meetings may be a onetime event, an event that takes course over several days or a series of events that take place over months or years. It all depends on the size of the group, the nature of the conflict or problem and the challenges associated with finding a solution the group can collectively support and champion. The process of facilitation includes the following:

- **Preparation:** Developing a pre-meeting agenda; surveying stakeholders to gain an understanding of the interests, goals, challenges and protocols, etc.
- **Convening:** Establishing meeting guidelines for participants and inviting input to ensure everyone's comfort level and utilizing various facilitation methods to achieve the greatest outcomes for a particular group
- **Follow up:** Preparing a meeting report that includes follow up duties

An important function of the facilitator is group maintenance, which involves:

- **Gatekeeping:** Inviting people to speak while strategically keeping others at bay as deemed necessary for the benefit of the group and its established goals
- **Harmonizing:** Calming the group, strategically minimizing and managing tensions and emotions as deemed necessary for the benefit of the group and its established goals

The facilitator provides feedback on how the group is functioning and makes suggestions and/or asks questions to find ways past impasse.

Upon conclusion of each meeting, the facilitator provides the meeting conveners with a report that includes the items covered during the meeting. It is a highly detailed report that includes an introduction and background section to bring context to the purpose of the facilitation; an explanation of the procedure, process and guidelines; as well as the transcription of all notes accumulated on flip-charts, white boards and other information gathering efforts. This report is used as the basis for determining next steps and what work will be included at the next meeting. If work needs to be done before the next meeting, the report will indicate those items as well.

World Café

World Café is an easy and flexible facilitation methodology for convening large group dialogue. World Café is a highly collaborative process, involving the active input of attendees. Named for the café-style of the environment set up, which includes round tables covered with butcher block paper, colored pens or pencils, a vase of flowers, and optional "talking stick" item. Depending on the nature of the dialogue, additional items may be included on the table to assist in the creative expression of the participants. The optimal size of each table is four to five participants.

The process opens with a welcome and introduction, in which the facilitator sets the context for the dialogue (i.e., why the parties are in attendance and what they are tasked with accomplishing). World Café etiquette and other grounds rules are presented. The process begins with the first of three (or more) 20-minute conversations that are held at each small table. The facilitator will provide the topic of the conversation or pose a question, but the goal of the first round is primarily to get comfortable with the process and begin a dialogue. At the end of the 20 minutes, each member of the group moves to a different table with one person staying behind as that table's host. The host welcomes the new group and updates them on what occurred in the previous round. The facilitator poses another question with the intent of progressing the dialogue. However, if more time is needed, the same questions may apply in multiple rounds. Between rounds, the facilitator may ask the groups to share insights or results from their conversations with the group at large. A person is tasked to be a scribe to record the insights and knowledge that is shared. This information is presented in the facilitator's report.

While World Café is just one way facilitators help groups resolve conflict or achieve consensus around a particular business issue, facilitation is a highly effective way to achieve resolutions to issues the group will buy-in to and comply with because their participation contributed to the creation of it. See the Appendix to learn more information about World Café.

REFRAME CONFLICT WITH RESTORATIVE JUSTICE

Restorative justice is a process for achieving justice that helps to restore the dignity of all people involved in a wrongdoing. It puts into place a framework for all people involved to have the opportunity to share in their mutual human development.

Restorative justice is most often associated with criminal justice as a framework for rethinking crime and punishment. The foundational principle of restorative justice is the care and respect of humanity. This means that when a wrong or harm has taken place, the respect for all individuals involved guides the process for making right the wrong.

In considering how to right the wrong, a restorative justice process takes into consideration the needs of the person or persons who was harmed, the individual(s) who created the harm, and their communities. The needs of the harmed person(s) are at the center of the justice process. The person who caused the harm is held accountable and responsible for righting the wrong and seeking opportunities for restitution. And the needs of the community are also included in the justice process. Restorative justice acknowledges that community members have roles to play in ensuring justice, and they may also have responsibilities to the individual who was harmed, the individual who created the harm and to themselves. Three principles shape a restorative justice process:

1. Crime (or a wrongdoing) is a violation of people and interpersonal relationships
2. Violations create obligations
3. The central obligation is to put right to the wrongs

The following table demonstrates the current view of achieving justice in a western criminal justice process as compared to a restorative justice process.

CRIMINAL JUSTICE	RESTORATIVE JUSTICE
• Crime is a violation of the law and the state.	• Crime is a violation of people and relationships.
• Violations create guilt.	• Violations create obligations.
• Justice requires the state to determine blame (guilt) and impose pain (punishment).	• Justice (i.e., to put things right) involves victims, offenders and community members.
Central focus: Offenders get what they deserve (i.e., punishment)	**Central focus:** Victim needs and offender responsibility for repairing harm

This table demonstrates the three questions each view seeks to answer:

CRIMINAL JUSTICE	RESTORATIVE JUSTICE
• What law has been broken?	• Who has been hurt?
• Who did it?	• What are their needs?
• What do they deserve?	• Whose obligations are these?

Implementing a restorative justice process in the workplace offers a similar point of view and asks similar questions. By simply reframing the criminal justice perspective to a workplace perspective, a new framework for managing workplace conflict emerges. The table below represents the current view of workplace conflict as compared to the restorative justice view.

TRADITIONAL PROCESS	RESTORATIVE JUSTICE
• Misconduct is a violation of policy and/or core values.	• Misconduct is a violation of people and relationships.
• Violations create guilt.	• Violations create obligations.
• Justice requires the state to determine blame (guilt) and impose pain (punishment).	• Justice (i.e., to put things right) involves all stakeholders in the conflict.
Central focus: Offending employees get what they deserve (i.e., punishment)	**Central focus:** Victim needs and the offending employee's repsonsibility for repairing the harm

By answering the following three questions, one can easily see how a restorative justice process optimizes employee engagement by placing the care of all individuals at the center of the conflict management process.

TRADITIONAL PROCESS	RESTORATIVE JUSTICE
• What policy or core value has been violated? • Who did it? • What do they deserve?	• Who has been harmed? • What is needed to repair the harm? • Whose obligation is it to repair the harm?

Managing complaints, grievances, policy and core values violations with a restorative justice model demonstrates to employees that their needs, their development and their concerns are respected by the workplace community and that opportunities for human growth and development exist. A restorative justice model for managing conflict deepens employee understanding of one another, instills trusts and therefore, increases employee engagement.

Restorative justice offers an effective and human-centric framework for managing workplace conflict. Engaging a third-party consultant proficient in restorative justice systems design who can develop a dispute resolution process specific to an organization's unique needs that is also consistent with its vision, mission and values and can help to bring about positive and lasting change. The following are several dialogue processes that are often utilized by restorative justice practitioners.

Conversation Cafés

Conversation Cafés are open conversations hosted by an individual within the organization or a third-party consultant. Anyone within an organization who wants to attend is invited to do so. Conversation Cafés are designed for inclusivity. The dialogue approach follows a simple process intended to address hard topics with integrity and fidelity. Conversations are one-and-a-half hours in length. The host asks the group stimulating questions framed to get at the heart of the matter. Anyone who wants to speak is invited to do so. The following core principles shape the Conversation Café process:[90]

- **Inclusivity:** Create an inviting environment in which all participants are inspired to speak and listen, and where diverse perspectives may emerge.
- **One host per table:** Ideally every table should have a host; however, if that is not possible there should be at least one person to host the event.
- **Open access:** Anyone may participate who follows the "rules" (See appendix).
- **Conversations are public domain:** What is said in a Conversation Café is not owned by anyone person and is considered to be in the public domain. No one at the table or outside the conversation may claim exclusive ownership of the ideas that emerge.
- **Commercial-free [and agenda-free] zones:** No one may attend primarily to promote a particular agenda, point of view, outcome, solution or cause.
- **No committees:** There will be no political networking, committee formation or action groups.

- **Empowering hosts:** Provide clear information to all hosts and participants about the mechanics of hosting a Conversation Café and the open, inquisitive spirit of hosting.
- **Maintaining integrity and fidelity:** Any event calling itself a Conversation Café must abide by the Conversation Café "Process and Agreements" (see Appendix) and principles. Borrowing from or altering these is encouraged, but such adaptations should not be called Conversation Cafés.

The Conversation Café process works well in the workplace because it empowers all individuals to participate in open and honest dialogue with clear ground rules established to preserve the integrity and dignity of the process, the dialogue and the individuals involved. When incorporating the principles of restorative justice, this style of dialogue enhances collaboration and creates opportunities for making connections in a heartfelt manner. See the Appendix to learn more about the Conversation Café process.

Dialogue Circles

A "dialogue circle" is a broad term that refers to a general methodology for exchanging narratives, gaining understanding of others' viewpoints, deepening connection and self-expressing in an honest and heartfelt way while receiving the self-expression of others with empathy and integrity. Dialogue circles can be used in formal and informal processes. The following are some examples of when a dialogue circle can be beneficial in the workplace:[91]

- Initial exploration of an organizational task
- Determining best practices
- Strategic planning
- Vision, mission and values initiatives
- Role clarifications and work responsibilities
- Procedural dilemmas in a "peace training" event
- Perceptions of the organization's "current reality"
- Team approaches to projects and plans
- Perceptions of the "other" in cultural competence training and personnel matters
- Organizational restructuring (and feelings about restructuring)

The sequence of a dialogue circle is as follows:

1. **Create a safe space for the dialogue.** This can be accomplished by opening with a moment of silence, an affirmation or something similar.
2. **Set guidelines for dialogue**. In a workplace environment, the group should establish ground rules and use these same ground rules each time a circle convenes. The circle can have an assigned facilitator or it could be self-facilitated by all members of the group. Sample ground rules include:
   - Speak from experience
   - Listen as equals
   - Suspend your assumptions
   - Respect the speaker
   - Defer the need for clarification
   - Focus on the learning

3. **Offer the question or issue for exploration.** Each circle should have a theme or topic that is in need of exploration. This could be a conflict that needs to be resolved or a business-related matter that needs to be addressed. The dialogue circle should always have a reason for convening.

4. **Share stories related to the question, issue or theme.** Stay on topic and use the time together respectfully, honoring the intent of the circle.

5. **Listen as colleagues and honor the person who is speaking.** Respecting what is heard and shared is of paramount importance to the effectiveness of dialogue circles as a vehicle for building peace in the workplace.

6. **Close the dialogue.** Explicitly state or mark the close of the dialogue session, shifting to discussion mode.

7. **Debrief the learning.** Discuss what was learned, what key takeaways will be and what next steps look like.

See the Appendix for more information on dialogue circles.

BECOME AN AGENT OF POSITIVE CHANGE WITH CONFLICT COACHING

Conflict coaching is a one-on-one training process designed to assist people in more effectively engaging in, managing and resolving conflict. A conflict coach works with an individual who is either experiencing conflict presently or is seeking to hone his or her conflict skills so as to navigate conflict more productively and effectively in the future. Similar to a life coach or business coach, a conflict coach provides a space for the individual to discuss a conflict (or conflict challenges) with a neutral third-party and explore ways to best manage the conflict, as well as develop an approach for discussing the conflict with the individual(s) involved. Conflict coaching is especially beneficial for individuals in management or leadership roles.

A conflict coach helps the individual perceive the conflict through various perspectives while providing support in identifying the best outcomes and options for achieving those outcomes. The conflict coach helps the individual achieve clarity about the situation and provides insights that can help the person make high-quality decisions to manage the conflict in the most productive manner — devising a plan and even rehearsing the conversation with the individual to ensure readiness.

Conflict coaching can be a transformative experience, helping individuals become agents of positive change by developing peaceful resolutions to conflict while preserving the integrity and dignity of those involved.

CONCLUSION

Putting peace into practice is truly where the rubber meets the road. Peace — human security and living a life of dignity that is free of fear — is a human right. Honoring that right in the workplace with an unwavering commitment from the organization and its leadership to contribute to humanity at the highest level and with the highest degree of integrity is not just what the best humans do, it is what the best businesses do. Peace is truly the birthplace of innovation and creativity for the very fact that it is the foundation of human security and dignity.

APPENDIX

CONFLICT MANAGEMENT AND DISPUTE RESOLUTION TRAINING

Corporate training in various topics are available through Robyn Short's alternative dispute resolution and training firm to assist groups and teams in deepening their trust and collaboration so they may increase performance as well as experience their contribution and value in more meaningful ways. Topics include, but are not limited to, the following:

The Neuroscience of Leadership. Effective leaders are highly emotionally intelligent and have a deep understanding of personal and social competence. In this training session, participants will gain an understanding of the brain — how it works and the role it plays in decision-making, as well as the four skills for developing or increasing emotional intelligence. Participants will learn how to increase their social and personal competence and learn why doing so is vital to effective leadership.

Conflict Management: When navigated effectively, conflict can be a valuable source of deepening relationships, improving trust and learning more about a person or a situation. However, when conflict is poorly managed, or not managed at all, it can have devastating consequences to relationships, teams and even entire organizations. To manage conflict effectively requires an understanding of one's self, an understanding of how the brain functions in conflict, communication and self-regulation techniques for managing conflict effectively, and a process for bringing these all together. Participants of this training session will gain a deeper understanding of conflict, the value conflict can bring to relationships and the skills necessary to reap those benefits. This training session can be tailored for the following audiences:

- Corporate environments
- Nonprofit staff and / or executive directors
- Families
- Academic students
- Academic faculty and staff
- Academic social clubs (sororities, fraternities, etc.)
- Law enforcement agencies
- Community agencies

How to Have Difficult Conversations: Difficult conversations are a necessary element of life — in both personal and professional settings. Too often, difficult conversations are avoided because people lack the understanding, and therefore confidence, to navigate difficult conversations productively. In this training session, participants will learn a step-by-step approach to having tough conversations, including how to:

- Structure a difficult conversation
- Communicate without putting anyone on the defense
- Listen for unspoken messages

- Remain calm in conflict
- Remain solutions-focused

This training session can be tailored for the following audiences:

- Corporate environments
- Nonprofit staff and / or executive directors
- Families
- Academic students
- Academic faculty and staff
- Academic social clubs (sororities, fraternities, etc.)
- Law enforcement agencies
- Community agencies

Interest-Based Negotiation: Too often, negotiations are perceived as a zero sum game — one person or group wins and the other loses. Effective negotiations that result in high rates of compliance seek to achieve win-win outcomes — outcomes that address underlying issues rather than perceived positions. This training session offers a step-by-step approach to gaining mutually acceptable agreements in both personal and professional disputes. Participants will gain confidence in their negotiation skills and will gain an understanding of the value in preserving both the relationship and the deal.

Peace in the Workplace: Peace is not the absence of conflict. Conflict will, and should, exist in human relationships. Peace is addressing conflict through nonviolent methods. This training session provides participants with the skills to: clarify what they are observing when in conflict; identify the emotions they are feeling when in conflict; and understand what to ask of themselves and others when in conflict. This training session will help participants illuminate paths to peace in the workplace through compassionate communication, increased understanding, deepening connections and, ultimately, the communication skills to resolve conflict.

Managing Workplace Conflict: Utilizing The Friendly Style Profile™ conflict assessment tool, attendees will gain an understanding of their conflict style during periods of calm and storm. Armed with this information and key insights on emotional intelligence traits and how to foster them, participants will learn communication strategies and tactics for effectively managing day-to-day workplace conflicts as well as high stakes conflicts. Experiential activities will help participants hone their conflict management skills and practice communication techniques with coworkers of the same and differing conflict styles. Participants will gain a deeper understanding of who they are in conflict and techniques for leveraging their innate conflict style.

Building High-Performing Teams: High performing teams are led by high impact leaders — leaders with the skills to create a culture that fosters the highest potential in every team member. In this training, participants will learn the characteristics of high impact leaders and behaviors that inspire others to achieve the vision set forth for the team. This session includes practical insights and exercises for becoming an inspiring leader and tactics for remaining present to the organization's mission and vision in high-pressure environments. Participants will gain actionable skills in leading high-performing teams.

View the current training schedule or learn about customized training for your organization: www.RobynShort.com.

WORLD CAFÉ

Learn more about World Café at www.theworldcafe.com.

CONVERSATION CAFÉ

Learn more about World Café at www.conversationcafe.org.

DIALOGUE CIRCLES

Learn more about World Café at www.dialogue-circles.com.

ABOUT THE AUTHOR

AN INTERNATIONAL SPEAKER, PEACE-BUILDING TRAINER and mediator, Robyn Short works with individuals, corporations and nonprofit organizations in discovering the root causes of their conflicts so they may transform their relationships and create new and productive paths forward individually and as teams. She also works with community leaders and political and governmental leaders to develop grassroots efforts for building sustainable peace in areas of historic conflict. In this capacity, she has been featured in news outlets internationally.

Robyn holds a Master of Arts in Conflict Management and Dispute Resolution from Southern Methodist University and a Master of Liberal Studies from Southern Methodist University with a focus in 15th century European history. She holds a B.S. in Psychology from Auburn University. Robyn is a practicing mediator with expertise in transformative mediation practices, victim/offender mediation and restorative justice. Learn more at www.RobynShort.com.

ACKNOWLEDGMENTS

FIRST AND FOREMOST, I am tremendously grateful to my partner Scott Mischnick, whose unwavering commitment to my work is both a source of inspiration and joy. I am tremendously grateful to the late Marshall Rosenberg whose pioneering work in the field of nonviolent communication has greatly influenced my work as well as the work of countless peacemakers. My colleagues, friends and mentors Kenneth Cloke and Betty Gilmore have served as both a lighthouse at times and a lifeboat at others. You both challenge me and inspire me. Thank you to Brooke Nottingham Howell, my friend and editor, who makes life better with her keen wit and books better with her keen eye and copy editing acumen. And perhaps most importantly, I am grateful to you, the reader, for choosing to be an agent of positive change in our shared human experience.

END NOTES

1   "Universal Declaration of Human Rights." Springer Reference (n.d.): n. pag. United Nations. United Nations. Web. 20 May 2016.

2   CPP Global Human Capital Report: Workplace Conflict and How Businesses Can Harness It to Thrive. Rep. Moutainview: CPP, 2008. Print.

3   Ibid.

4   Tattersall, Ian. The World from Beginnings to 4000 BCE. Oxford: Oxford University Press, 2008.

5   Fine, Cordelia. *The Britannica Guide to the Brain: A Guided Tour of the Brain - Mind, Memory, and Intelligence.* London: Robinson, 2008.

6   Ibid.

7   Ibid.

8   Ibid.

9   Ibid.

10   Ibid.

11   Ibid.

12   Ibid.

13   Ibid.

14   Ibid.

15   Ibid.

16   Ibid.

17   Cloke, Ken. *The Dance of Opposites: Explorations in Mediation, Dialogue and Conflict Resolution Systems Design.* Dallas: GoodMedia Press, 2014.

18   Perry, Susan. "Mirror Neurons." Brain Facts. February 2, 2013. Accessed January 10, 2015.

19   Gilmore, Betty, Dr. "Neuroscience of Collaboration, and Attachment." Lecture, Neuroscience of Collaboration, and Attachment, Southern Methodist University, Plano, 2012.

20   "The Brain From Top to Bottom." The Brain From Top to Bottom. Accessed January 10, 2016. http://thebrain.mcgill. ca/flash/a/a_04/a_04_cr/a_04_cr_peu/a_04_cr_peu.html.
   Gilmore, Betty, Dr. "Neuroscience of Conflict." Lecture, Neuroscience of Conflict, Southern Methodist University, Plano, 2012.

21   Ibid.

22   "The Brain From Top to Bottom." The Brain From Top to Bottom. Accessed January 10, 2016. http://thebrain.mcgill. ca/flash/a/a_04/a_04_cr/a_04_cr_peu/a_04_cr_peu.html.

23   Cloke, Ken. *The Dance of Opposites: Explorations in Mediation, Dialogue and Conflict Resolution Systems Design.* Dallas: GoodMedia Press, 2014.

24   DeAngelis, Tori. "The Two Faces of Oxytocin." *Monitor on Psychology* 39, no. 2 (February 2008): 30. Accessed January

10, 2016. http://www.apa.org/monitor/feb08/oxytocin.aspx.

25   "The Brain From Top to Bottom." The Brain From Top to Bottom. Accessed January 10, 2016. http://thebrain.mcgill. ca/flash/a/a_04/a_04_cr/a_04_cr_peu/a_04_cr_peu.html.

26   DeAngelis, Tori. "The Two Faces of Oxytocin." *Monitor on Psychology* 39, no. 2 (February 2008): 30. Accessed January 10, 2016. http://www.apa.org/monitor/feb08/oxytocin.aspx.

27   Ibid.

28   Cloke, Ken. *The Dance of Opposites: Explorations in Mediation, Dialogue and Conflict Resolution Systems Design*. Dallas: GoodMedia Press, 2014.

29   Coleman, Daniel. "Three Kinds of Empathy: Cognitive, Emotional, Compassionate." Danial Goleman. June 12, 2007. Accessed January 10, 2016. http://www.danielgoleman.info/ three-kinds-of-empathy-cognitive-emotional-compassionate.

30   Cloke, Ken. *The Dance of Opposites: Explorations in Mediation, Dialogue and Conflict Resolution Systems Design*. Dallas: GoodMedia Press, 2014.

31   Schaufenbuel, Kimberly. "Why Google, Target, and General Mills Are Investing in Mindfulness." *Harvard Business Review*. Www.hbr.org, 28 Dec. 2015. Web. 21 May 2016.

32   Liu, Xinghua, Wei Xu, Yuzheng Wang, Mark G. Williamson, Yan Geng, Qian Zhang, and Xin Liu. "Can Inner Peace Be Improved by Mindfulness Training:A Randomized Controlled Trial." Wiley Online Library. March 7, 2013. Accessed November 23, 2015. doi:10.1002/smi.2551.

33   Ibid.

34   Ibid.

35   Cloke, Ken, and Joan Goldsmith. *Resolving Conflicts at Work: Ten Strategies for Everyone on the Job*. San Francisco: Jossey-Bass, 2011. Print.

36   Thomas, Kenneth W., and Ralph H. Kilmann. "An Overview of the Thomas-Kilmann Conflict Mode Instrument (TKI)." *An Overview of the TKI*. Kilmann Diagnostics, n.d. Web. 28 May 2016. <http://www.kilmanndiagnostics.com/ overview-thomas-kilmann-conflict-mode-instrument-tki>.

37   Ibid.

38   Cloke, Ken, and Joan Goldsmith. *Resolving Conflicts at Work: Ten Strategies for Everyone on the Job*. San Francisco: Jossey-Bass, 2011. Print.

39   Rosenberg, Marshall B. *Nonviolent Communication: A Language of Life*. Encinitas: PuddleDancer, 2015. Print.

40   Ibid.

41   CPP Global Human Capital Report: Workplace Conflict and How Businesses Can Harness It to Thrive. Rep. Moutainview: CPP, 2008. Print.

42   *CPP Global Human Capital Report: Workplace Conflict and How Businesses Can Harness It to Thrive*. Rep. Moutainview: CPP, 2008. Print.

43   Rosenberg, Marshall B. *Nonviolent Communication: A Language of Life*. Encinitas: PuddleDancer, 2015. Print.

44   Brafman, Ori, and Rom Brafman. *Sway: The Irresistible*

Pull of Irrational Behavior. New York: Doubleday, 2008. Print.

45   Rosenberg, Marshall B. *Nonviolent Communication: A Language of Life*. Encinitas: PuddleDancer, 2015. Print.

46   Brown, Brené, PhD. "The Power of Vulnerability." TEDxHouston. Houston. June 2010. *TED*. Web. 23 May 2016.   <https://www.ted.com/talks/brene_brown_on_vulnerability?language=en>.

47   Rosenberg, Marshall B. *Nonviolent Communication: A Language of Life*. Encinitas: PuddleDancer, 2015. Print.

48   Ibid.

49   Ibid.

50   Ibid.

51   Frankl, Viktor E. *Man's Search for Meaning*. Boston: Beacon, 2006. Print.

52   Rosenberg, Marshall B. *Nonviolent Communication: A Language of Life*. Encinitas: PuddleDancer, 2015. Print.

53   Ibid.

54   Ibid.

55   *014 WBI U.S. Workplace Bullying Survey*. Rep. Workplace Bullying Institute, 2014. Web. 2 June 2016. <http://workplacebullying.org/multi/pdf/2014-Survey-Flyer-A.pdf>.

56   Ibid.

57   Kilmann, Ralph H. "Bullying Behavior and Conflict

Management." *Online Courses for Conflict Management and Change Management.* Kilmann Diagnostics, n.d. Web. 02 June 2016. <http://www.kilmanndiagnostics.com/blog/2012/apr/10/bullying-behavior-and-conflict-management>.

58   *2014 WBI U.S. Workplace Bullying Survey.* Rep. Workplace Bullying Institute, 2014. Web. 2 June 2016. <http://workplacebullying.org/multi/pdf/2014-Survey-Flyer-A.pdf>.

59   Namie, Ruth, PhD, and Gary Namie, PhD. "Employer Resource Council: 20 Subtle Signs of Workplace Bullying." *Workplace Bullying Institute RSS*. Workplace Bullying Institute, n.d. Web. 04 June 2016. <http://www.workplacebullying.org/erc/>.

60   Namie, Ruth, PhD, and Gary Namie, PhD. " How Bullying Can Affect Your Brain and Body." *Workplace Bullying Institute RSS*. Workplace Bullying Institute, n.d. Web. 02 June 2016.   <http://www.workplacebullying.org/individuals/impact/physical-health-harm/>.

61   Williams, Kipling D. "Ostracism." *Psychology Annual Review of Psychology* 58 (2007): 426-44. Web. 4 June 2016.

62   Ibid.

63   Namie, Ruth, PhD, and Gary Namie, PhD. " ." *Workplace Bullying Institute RSS*. Workplace Bullying Institute, n.d. Web. 04 June 2016. <http://www.workplacebullying.org/individuals/impact/social-harm/>.

64   Namie, Ruth, PhD, and Gary Namie, PhD. " Economic Harm." *Workplace Bullying Institute RSS*. Workplace Bullying Institute, n.d. Web. 04 June 2016. <http://www.workplacebullying.org/individuals/impact/economic-harm/>.

65   Namie, Ruth, PhD, and Gary Namie, PhD. " Impact of Workplace Bullying on Coworkers." *Workplace Bullying Institute RSS*. Workplace Bullying Institute, n.d. Web. 04 June 2016.   <http://www.workplacebullying.org/individuals/impact/coworkers/>.

66   Namie, Ruth F., PhD, and Gary Namie, PhD. " Who Gets Targeted." *Workplace Bullying Institute*. Workplace Bullying Institute, n.d. Web. 02 June 2016. <http://www.workplacebullying.org/individuals/problem/who-gets-targeted/>.

67   Ury, W., & Ury, W. (2000). *The Third Side: Why we fight and how we can stop*. New York: Penguin Books.

68   Gilmore, Betty, Dr. "Neuroscience of Conflict." Lecture, Neuroscience of Conflict, Southern Methodist University, Plano, 2012.

69   Power-point by: Mark McKenna; BUS 162 (6), International and Comparative Management: The Role of Cross- Cultural Communication and Negotiation ; San Jose State University; *Intercultural Business Communication*. Retrieved from Kwintessential Cross Cultural Solutions

70   Lewis, Richard D. When Cultures Collide: Managing Successfully across Cultures. London: N. Brealey Pub., 1996. Print.

71   Meierding, Nina. "Gender, Culture and Conflict." Gender, Culture and Conflict Graduate Course. Southern Methodist University, Plano. 13 May 2012. Lecture.

72   Gilmore, Betty, Psy. "Non-verbal Communication: Essentials for Mediators." Conflict Resolution Network. Plano.

25 July 2016. Lecture.

73   Ibid.

74   Tannen, Deborah. Talking from 9 to 5: How Women's and Men's Conversational Styles Affect Who Gets Heard, Who Gets Credit, and What Gets Done at Work. New York: W. Morrow, 1994. Print.

75   Meierding, Nina, and Jan Frankel Shau. "Negotiating Like a Woman: How Gender Impacts Communication Between the Sexes Ritual." Mediate. Mediate.com, n.d. Web. 25 July 2016. <http://www.mediate.com/articles/SchauMeierding. cfm>.

76   "Equal Employment Opportunity Commission." LII / Legal Information Institute. N.p., n.d. Web. 25 July 2016. <https://www.law.cornell.edu/wex/equal_employment_ opportunity_commission>.

77   Abreu, Kimberly. "The Myriad Benefits of Diversity in the Workplace." Entrepreneur. Entrepreneur.com, 08 Dec. 2014. Web. 25 July 2016. <https://www.entrepreneur.com/ article/240550>.

78   "What Is Apple's Current Mission Statement and How Does It Differ from Steve Job's Original Ideals? | Investopedia." Investopedia. N.p., 23 Apr. 2015. Web. 27 July 2016. <http:// www.investopedia.com/ask/answers/042315/what-apples- current-mission-statement-and-how-does-it-differ-steve- jobs-original-ideals.asp>.

79   Ibid.

80   Cuthbertson, Anthony. "Apple IPhone 6s Factory's 'toxic' Conditions Exposed in New Undercover Investigation."

International Business Times RSS. International Business Times, 22 Oct. 2015. Web. 31 July 2016. <http://www.ibtimes. co.uk/iphone-6s-factory-investigation-reveals-apple-still-violates-human-rights-workers-1525151>.

81   Gallo, Carmine. The Innovation Secrets of Steve Jobs: Insanely Different: Principles for Breakthrough Success. New York: McGraw-Hill, 2011. Print.

82   "Apple's Vision Statement & Mission Statement - Panmore Institute." Panmore Institute. N.p., 03 Sept. 2015. Web. 27 July 2016. <http://panmore.com/apple-mission-statement-vision-statement>.

83   Austin, Sam. "Two Years After Steve Jobs' Death, Is Apple a Different Company? | TIME.com." Business Money Two Years After Steve Jobs Death Is Apple a Different Company Comments. Time Magazine, 4 Oct. 2013. Web. 28 July 2016. <http://business.time.com/2013/10/04/two-years-after-steve-jobs-death-is-apple-a-different-company/>.

84   Lencioni, Patrick. "Make Your Values Mean Something." Harvard Business Review. Harvard Business Review, 01 July 2002. Web. 28 July 2016. <https://hbr.org/2002/07/make-your-values-mean-something>.

85   Ibid.

86   CPP Global Human Capital Report: Workplace Conflict and How Businesses Can Harness It to Thrive. Rep. Moutainview: CPP, 2008. Print.

87   Ibid.

88   Ibid.

89   Ibid.

90   "Principles for Conversation Cafés." Conversation Cafes. Conversation Cafes, n.d. Web. 29 July 2016. <http://www.conversationcafe.org/principles-for-conversation-cafes/>.

91   "Dialogue's Uses." Dialogue Circles. Dialogue Circles, n.d. Web. 29 July 2016. <http://www.dialogue-circles.com/?page_id=122>.